THE BIG
THE ULTIMATE

NEW YORK CITY

TRAVEL GUIDE

DIANA L. MITCHELL

© **Copyright 2024 - All rights reserved.**

The content contained within this book may not be reproduced, duplicated or transmitted without direct written permission from the author or the publisher.

Under no circumstances will any blame or legal responsibility be held against the publisher, or author, for any damages, reparation, or monetary loss due to the information contained within this book, either directly or indirectly.

Legal Notice:

This book is copyright protected. It is only for personal use. You cannot amend, distribute, sell, use, quote or paraphrase any part, or the content within this book, without the consent of the author or publisher.

Disclaimer Notice:

Please note the information contained within this document is for educational and entertainment purposes only. All effort has been executed to present accurate, up to date, reliable, complete information. No warranties of any kind are declared or implied. Readers acknowledge that the author is not engaged in the rendering of legal, financial, medical or professional advice. The content within this book has been derived from various sources. Please consult a licensed professional before attempting any techniques outlined in this book.

By reading this document, the reader agrees that under no circumstances is the author responsible for any losses, direct or indirect, that are incurred as a result of the use of the information contained within this document, including, but not limited to, errors, omissions, or inaccuracies.

Cover image: © Tanarch / Getty Images via canva.com

Dear reader, thanks a lot for purchasing my book.

To help you plan your trip even more efficiently, I have included an interactive map powered by Google My Maps.

To access it, scan the QR code below.

Happy travelling!

A Note to Our Valued Readers

Thank you for choosing this travel guide as your companion for exploring the world.

I want to take a moment to address a concern you might have regarding the absence of photographs in this book.

As an independent author and publisher, I strive to deliver high-quality, informative content at an affordable price.

Including photographs in a printed book, however, presents significant challenges. Licensing high-quality images can be extremely costly, and unfortunately, I have no control over the print quality of images within the book.

Because these guides are printed and shipped by Amazon, I am unable to review the final print quality before they reach your hands.

So, rather than risk compromising your reading experience with subpar visuals, I've chosen to focus on providing detailed, insightful content that will help you make the most of your travels.

While this guide may not contain photos, it's packed with valuable information, insider tips, and recommendations to ensure you have an enriching and memorable journey.

Additionally, there's an interactive map powered by Google My Maps—an essential tool to help you plan your trip.

I encourage you to supplement your reading with online resources where you can find up-to-date images and visuals of the destinations covered in this guide.

I hope you find this book a helpful and inspiring resource as you embark on your next adventure.

Thank you for your understanding and support.

Safe travels,

Diana

Table of Contents

Welcome to New York City 1
   Why visit NYC? 1
      Iconic Landmarks 2
      Cultural Diversity 2
      World-Class Museums and Art 2
      Broadway and Entertainment 2
      Culinary Delights 3
      Shopping Mecca 3
      Green Spaces and Recreation 3
      Historical Significance 3
      Vibrant Neighborhoods 3
      Year-Round Attractions 4
Getting Around 5
   Public Transportation 5
      Subway System 5
      Bus Routes 6
      Staten Island Ferry 7
   Taxis and Rideshares 8
      Yellow Cabs 8
      Uber and Lyft 9
   Biking 11
      Citi Bike program 11
What to See and Do 13
   Iconic Landmarks 13
      Statue of Liberty 13
      Empire State Building 14
      Times Square 15

Central Park 16
Brooklyn Bridge 17
Rockefeller Center 18
Chrysler Building 19
One World Trade Center (Freedom Tower) 20
Fifth Avenue 21
Grand Central Terminal 22
Bryant Park 23

Museums and Cultural Institutions 25
    The Metropolitan Museum of Art 25
    Museum of Modern Art (MoMA) 26
    American Museum of Natural History 27
    Guggenheim Museum 28
    Whitney Museum of American Art 29
    The Frick Collection 30
    New-York Historical Society 31
    Museum of the City of New York 32
    Intrepid Sea, Air & Space Museum 33
    The Morgan Library & Museum 34

Theaters and Performances 37
    Broadway Theaters (collective) 37
    Radio City Music Hall 38
    Lincoln Center for the Performing Arts 39
    Carnegie Hall 40
    The Public Theater 41
    Apollo Theater 42
    Beacon Theatre 43
    New Amsterdam Theatre 44

Gershwin Theatre	45
St. James Theatre	46
Historic Sites	**49**
Ellis Island	49
9/11 Memorial & Museum	50
St. Patrick's Cathedral	51
Trinity Church	52
Flatiron Building	53
New York Public Library (Main Branch)	54
United Nations Headquarters	55
Federal Hall	56
Fraunces Tavern Museum	57
Brooklyn Historical Society	58
Observation Decks	**61**
Top of the Rock Observation Deck	61
Empire State Building Observatory	62
One World Observatory	63
Edge at Hudson Yards	64
The High Line	65
Roosevelt Island Tramway	66
Summit One Vanderbilt	67
Brooklyn Heights Promenade	68
Liberty State Park (views of Manhattan skyline)	69
Neighborhood Exploration	**71**
Greenwich Village	71
SoHo	72
Harlem	73
Williamsburg	74

- Chinatown 75
- Little Italy 76
- Upper West Side 77
- East Village 77
- DUMBO 78
- Astoria 79

Food and Dining 81
Iconic NYC Foods 81
- Bagels 81
- Pizza 82
- Hot Dogs 82

Fine Dining 83
- Michelin-Starred Restaurants 83
- Internationally Inspired Fine Dining 84

Casual Eateries 84
- Neighborhood Favorites 84
- Trendy Cafes and Diners 85

Street Food and Food Trucks 85
- Classic Street Food 86
- Gourmet Food Trucks 86
- Pop-Up Markets 86

Ethnic Cuisine 87
- Little Italy 87
- Chinatown 88
- Koreatown 88

Food Markets 89
- Chelsea Market 90
- Smorgasburg 90

Welcome to New York City

Welcome to New York City, a vibrant metropolis known as the "City That Never Sleeps." Bursting with energy and excitement, NYC is a melting pot of cultures, cuisines, and experiences, making it one of the most dynamic cities in the world. Whether you're a first-time visitor or a seasoned traveler, the city's iconic skyline, diverse neighborhoods, and rich history offer endless opportunities for exploration and adventure.

New York City is composed of five boroughs—Manhattan, Brooklyn, Queens, The Bronx, and Staten Island—each with its unique character and charm. From the towering skyscrapers of Manhattan to the artistic enclaves of Brooklyn, the multicultural mosaic of Queens, the historic sites of The Bronx, and the serene parks of Staten Island, there's something for everyone in NYC.

The city is home to some of the world's most famous landmarks, such as the Statue of Liberty, Empire State Building, and Times Square. It's a global hub for arts, culture, and entertainment, boasting world-class museums, theaters, and music venues. Whether you're strolling through Central Park, catching a Broadway show, exploring trendy neighborhoods, or savoring culinary delights from around the globe, New York City promises an unforgettable experience.

Join us as we guide you through the best of what NYC has to offer, providing tips and insights to help you make the most of your visit to this extraordinary city.

Why visit NYC?

New York City is a destination like no other, offering a unique blend of history, culture, and modernity that captivates millions of visitors each year. Here are some compelling reasons why NYC should be at the top of your travel list:

Iconic Landmarks

NYC is home to some of the world's most recognizable landmarks. From the towering Statue of Liberty, symbolizing freedom and democracy, to the breathtaking views from the Empire State Building and the bustling energy of Times Square, these iconic sites are must-sees for any visitor.

Cultural Diversity

New York City is a true melting pot, with over 800 languages spoken and an incredibly diverse population. This cultural richness is reflected in the city's neighborhoods, festivals, and culinary scene, offering a global experience without leaving the city.

World-Class Museums and Art

Art enthusiasts will find paradise in NYC, with its array of world-renowned museums and galleries. The Metropolitan Museum of Art, the Museum of Modern Art (MoMA), and the Guggenheim Museum showcase masterpieces from around the world, while countless smaller galleries and cultural institutions offer a deeper dive into various art forms and historical periods.

Broadway and Entertainment

Theater lovers flock to NYC for its vibrant Broadway scene. With an array of shows, from classic musicals to cutting-edge plays, there's always something new and exciting to see. Beyond Broadway, the city's comedy clubs, live music venues, and performance spaces ensure endless entertainment options.

Culinary Delights

New York City's food scene is legendary, offering everything from Michelin-starred fine dining to iconic street food. Indulge in a slice of authentic New York pizza, savor international cuisines in diverse neighborhoods, or explore food markets like Chelsea Market and Smorgasburg for a true culinary adventure.

Shopping Mecca

NYC is a shopper's paradise, featuring luxury boutiques on Fifth Avenue, trendy shops in SoHo, and unique finds in street markets. Whether you're looking for high-end fashion, vintage treasures, or quirky souvenirs, the city has it all.

Green Spaces and Recreation

Amidst the urban hustle, NYC boasts beautiful parks and green spaces. Central Park offers a serene escape with its meadows, lakes, and walking trails, while smaller parks like Bryant Park and the High Line provide unique urban oases.

Historical Significance

With its rich history, NYC offers numerous sites of historical importance. Explore Ellis Island and the 9/11 Memorial to gain insights into the city's past and its role in shaping modern America.

Vibrant Neighborhoods

Each NYC neighborhood has its distinct character and charm. From the artistic vibes of Greenwich Village and the upscale allure of the Upper East Side to the hipster haven of Williamsburg and the historic streets of Harlem, there's always a new area to discover.

Year-Round Attractions

No matter the season, NYC offers a plethora of activities and events. Enjoy summer concerts in the park, fall foliage in Central Park, winter ice skating at Rockefeller Center, and spring blooms at the New York Botanical Garden.

New York City's dynamic spirit, cultural depth, and endless possibilities make it an unforgettable destination for travelers from around the world. Whether you're here for a weekend or an extended stay, NYC promises experiences that will leave you wanting to return time and again.

Getting Around

Public Transportation

New York City boasts an extensive and efficient public transportation system, making it easy to navigate the city without a car. Here's an overview of the key public transportation options, including the subway system, bus routes, and the Staten Island Ferry.

Subway System

Overview:
- The NYC subway system is one of the largest and oldest public transit systems in the world, with 472 stations across four boroughs: Manhattan, Brooklyn, Queens, and the Bronx.
- Operated by the Metropolitan Transportation Authority (MTA), the subway runs 24/7, providing a convenient and reliable mode of transportation for millions of residents and visitors.

Subway Lines:
- The subway system consists of 27 lines, each identified by either a letter or number (e.g., A, C, E, 1, 2, 3).
- Lines are color-coded based on the route they follow (e.g., blue for the A, C, E lines; red for the 1, 2, 3 lines).
- Trains typically run local or express; local trains stop at every station, while express trains skip certain stations for faster travel.

Using the Subway:
- **MetroCard:** The standard fare payment method. Purchase and reload at station vending machines or booths. Pay-per-ride and unlimited ride options are available.
- **OMNY:** A new contactless payment system being rolled out across the subway and bus systems. Tap your contactless card or device at the turnstile to pay.

- **Maps and Apps:** Subway maps are available in stations and online. Apps like MTA Subway Time and Citymapper provide real-time updates and route planning.
- **Safety Tips:** Stay aware of your surroundings, avoid empty cars, and keep belongings secure. Use staffed entrances and exits, especially late at night.

Key Stations:
- **Times Square-42nd Street:** Major transfer point for multiple lines.
- **Grand Central-42nd Street:** Connects to Metro-North Railroad.
- **Penn Station-34th Street:** Connects to Amtrak, LIRR, and NJ Transit.
- **Fulton Street:** Major hub in Lower Manhattan, connecting several lines.
- **Union Square-14th Street:** Key transfer station in downtown Manhattan.

Bus Routes

Overview:
- NYC's bus system complements the subway, providing access to areas not well-served by trains.
- Buses operate throughout all five boroughs, with more than 300 routes, including local, express, and Select Bus Service (SBS).

Types of Buses:
- Local Buses: Make frequent stops, serving specific neighborhoods and routes.
- Express Buses: Provide faster service with fewer stops, primarily catering to commuters traveling between boroughs and Manhattan.
- Select Bus Service (SBS): Offers faster service with dedicated bus lanes, fewer stops, and off-board fare payment.

Using the Bus:
- MetroCard/OMNY: Same fare payment methods as the subway. MetroCards can be swiped or tapped on the farebox; OMNY users tap their contactless card or device.

- Bus Stops: Look for blue and white signs with route numbers. Check schedules and maps posted at stops or use transit apps for real-time information.
- Boarding: Enter through the front door and exit through the rear door (except on SBS, where all doors can be used for boarding and exiting).

Popular Routes:
- **M15 SBS:** Runs along First and Second Avenues in Manhattan, offering quick north-south travel.
- **B41:** Connects Downtown Brooklyn to southern Brooklyn neighborhoods like Flatbush and Kings Plaza.
- **Q60:** Travels along Queens Boulevard, connecting Jamaica to Midtown Manhattan.
- **Bx12 SBS:** Crosses the Bronx from east to west, providing rapid transit along Fordham Road and Pelham Parkway.

Staten Island Ferry

Overview:
- The Staten Island Ferry provides a vital link between Staten Island and Manhattan, operating since 1905.
- It is a free service, running 24/7, transporting over 22 million passengers annually.

Route and Schedule:
- Route: The ferry travels between the Whitehall Terminal in Lower Manhattan and the St. George Terminal on Staten Island.
- Schedule: Ferries run every 15-30 minutes during peak hours and every 30-60 minutes during off-peak hours. Check the ferry schedule online for exact times.

Experience:
- Scenic Views: Enjoy stunning views of the Statue of Liberty, Ellis Island, and the Manhattan skyline.
- Amenities: Terminals offer various amenities, including food and beverage options, restrooms, and waiting areas.
- Accessibility: Both terminals and ferries are fully accessible for passengers with disabilities.

Connecting Transportation:
- Whitehall Terminal: Access to multiple subway lines (1, R, W, 4, 5), buses, and the NYC Ferry service.
- St. George Terminal: Connections to Staten Island buses and the Staten Island Railway, providing further access across Staten Island.

New York City's public transportation system is extensive and user-friendly, making it easy to get around the city efficiently. Whether you're taking the subway, riding the bus, or enjoying a scenic trip on the Staten Island Ferry, you'll find a range of options to suit your travel needs.

Taxis and Rideshares

New York City offers a variety of taxi and rideshare options that provide convenient and flexible transportation throughout the five boroughs. Here's a detailed look at yellow cabs, Uber, and Lyft, including how to use them, fare information, and tips for a smooth ride.

Yellow Cabs

Overview:
- The iconic yellow cabs are synonymous with NYC and are regulated by the New York City Taxi and Limousine Commission (TLC).
- They can be hailed on the street or found at taxi stands throughout the city.

How to Hail a Yellow Cab:
- Street Hailing: Stand on the curb and raise your arm when you see an available cab. An available cab's roof light will be illuminated.
- Taxi Stands: Often located near major hotels, transportation hubs, and popular attractions.
- Telephone Dispatch: Some yellow cab companies offer phone dispatch services, but this is less common than street hailing.

Fare Information:
- Base Fare: Starts at $3.30, with additional charges based on distance and time.
- Surcharges: Night surcharge (8 PM - 6 AM) of $1 and a rush hour surcharge (4 PM - 8 PM weekdays) of $2.50.
- Tolls: Any bridge or tunnel tolls are added to the fare.
- Tips: A customary tip for taxi drivers is 15-20% of the total fare.
- Payment: Accepted in cash and credit/debit cards. All cabs are equipped with card readers.

Tips for a Smooth Ride:
- Provide Clear Directions: Have your destination address ready and communicate it clearly to the driver.
- Safety: Make sure the taxi's medallion number and driver's information are displayed on the dashboard.
- Receipt: Always ask for a receipt at the end of your ride for record-keeping or in case you need to retrieve lost items.

Uber and Lyft

Overview:
- Uber and Lyft are popular rideshare services in NYC, offering convenient, app-based transportation options.
- These services provide a range of vehicle types, from budget-friendly rides to luxury options.

Using Uber and Lyft:
- Download the App: Available on both iOS and Android platforms.
- Create an Account: Sign up with your email, phone number, and payment information.
- Request a Ride: Enter your destination and choose the type of ride (e.g., UberX, UberPOOL, Lyft, Lyft XL).
- Track Your Ride: The app provides real-time tracking of your driver's location and estimated arrival time.
- Payment: Automatically charged to your registered payment method. Tips can be added through the app.

Fare Information:
- Base Fare: Varies by service type and time of day.

- Surge Pricing: During peak times or high demand, prices may increase due to surge pricing.
- Tolls: Any applicable bridge or tunnel tolls are added to the fare.
- Tips: Tipping is optional but appreciated and can be done through the app.

Service Options:
- UberX/Lyft: Standard ride for up to four passengers.
- UberPOOL/Lyft Shared: Shared rides with other passengers heading in the same direction, offering a lower fare.
- UberXL/Lyft XL: Larger vehicles for groups up to six passengers.
- Uber Black/Lyft Lux: Premium black car service for a more luxurious ride experience.

Tips for a Smooth Ride:
- Confirm Your Ride: Verify the driver's name, vehicle make, model, and license plate before getting in.
- Safety Features: Both apps offer safety features such as sharing your trip status with friends and family and in-app emergency assistance.
- Pickup Locations: Choose a safe and convenient pickup location, especially in busy areas.
- Ratings: Rate your driver after the ride to provide feedback on your experience.

Comparisons and Considerations
- Availability: Yellow cabs are typically more abundant in high-traffic areas like Midtown Manhattan, while rideshare services can be more convenient in outer boroughs or less busy neighborhoods.
- Cost: Rideshare fares can be more variable due to surge pricing, whereas yellow cab fares are more consistent but may include surcharges during peak times.
- Convenience: Rideshare apps offer the convenience of cashless payment and real-time tracking, while yellow cabs can be easily hailed on the street without the need for an app.

Whether you choose the traditional yellow cab or a modern rideshare service like Uber or Lyft, New York City provides a range of options to suit your transportation needs. Understanding how to use these services effectively can help you navigate the city with ease and make the most of your time in NYC.

Biking

Citi Bike program

Overview:
- Citi Bike is New York City's bike-sharing system, offering a convenient and eco-friendly way to get around the city.
- Launched in 2013, it has grown to include thousands of bikes and hundreds of stations across Manhattan, Brooklyn, Queens, the Bronx, and Jersey City.

How Citi Bike Works:
- Membership Options: Choose from various membership plans, including Single Ride, Day Pass, and Annual Membership.
    - Single Ride: Best for occasional users, allows a 30-minute ride for a fixed fee.
    - Day Pass: Ideal for tourists, offers unlimited 30-minute rides in a 24-hour period.
    - Annual Membership: Best for residents, includes unlimited 45-minute rides for a year.
- Finding a Bike: Use the Citi Bike app or website to locate nearby stations and check bike availability.
- Unlocking a Bike: Use the app, your Citi Bike key (for annual members), or a ride code to unlock a bike at any station.
- Riding and Returning: Enjoy your ride and return the bike to any Citi Bike station. Make sure the bike is securely docked to end your ride.

Benefits of Using Citi Bike:
- Flexibility: Easily navigate through traffic and access areas not well-served by public transportation.
- Health and Fitness: Enjoy a workout while commuting or sightseeing.
- Environmentally Friendly: Reduce your carbon footprint by opting for a bike over a car or taxi.

Tips for a Smooth Ride:
- Plan Your Route: Use the Citi Bike app to plan safe and efficient routes.

- Follow Traffic Rules: Obey all traffic signals and signs, use bike lanes where available, and signal your turns.
- Safety Gear: Always wear a helmet and consider using reflective clothing or lights, especially at night.
- Station Availability: Check the app for docking station availability near your destination to avoid last-minute hassles.

Popular Routes and Destinations:
- Central Park Loop: Enjoy a scenic ride through Central Park's bike-friendly paths.
- Hudson River Greenway: Ride along the west side of Manhattan with beautiful river views.
- Brooklyn Bridge: Experience the iconic bridge on two wheels and explore Brooklyn.

What to See and Do

Iconic Landmarks

Statue of Liberty

The Statue of Liberty, a towering symbol of freedom and democracy, stands majestically on Liberty Island in New York Harbor. Designed by French sculptor Frédéric Auguste Bartholdi and gifted to the United States by France in 1886, the statue commemorates the centennial of American independence and symbolizes the enduring friendship between the two nations. At 305 feet tall, including its pedestal, Lady Liberty is an iconic figure recognized worldwide.

Visitors to the Statue of Liberty begin their journey with a ferry ride from Battery Park in Manhattan or Liberty State Park in New Jersey. The scenic voyage offers stunning views of the New York City skyline and the harbor. Upon arriving on Liberty Island, guests can explore the grounds and take in the statue's grandeur from various vantage points.

The Statue of Liberty Museum, located on the island, provides a comprehensive history of the statue's creation, construction, and symbolism. Interactive exhibits and artifacts, including Bartholdi's original torch, offer deep insights into the statue's significance. The museum also features a theater where visitors can watch a short film about the statue's history.

For those seeking a more immersive experience, a climb to the crown of the Statue of Liberty offers unparalleled views. The ascent involves climbing 354 steps from the pedestal to the crown, providing a unique perspective on the statue's intricate design and the breathtaking panorama of New York Harbor.

The pedestal itself, accessible via an elevator or stairs, houses additional exhibits and provides a sweeping view from its observation deck. The statue's base is inscribed with Emma Lazarus's famous sonnet, "The New Colossus," which welcomes immigrants with the words, "Give me your tired, your poor, your huddled masses yearning to breathe free."

A visit to the Statue of Liberty is not just a sightseeing excursion but a profound journey into America's heritage and ideals. It stands as a powerful reminder of the nation's commitment to liberty and justice for all, making it a must-visit destination for anyone exploring New York City.

Empire State Building

The Empire State Building, an Art Deco masterpiece and an enduring symbol of New York City, soars 1,454 feet above Midtown Manhattan. Completed in 1931 during the Great Depression, it was the tallest building in the world until 1970 and remains one of the city's most iconic landmarks. Designed by William F. Lamb, the building's sleek design and rapid construction—completed in just over a year—are testaments to American ingenuity and ambition.

Visitors to the Empire State Building begin their experience in the grand lobby, which features stunning Art Deco design elements and murals depicting the building as the Eighth Wonder of the World. The lobby sets the stage for the journey upward, combining elegance with the excitement of visiting one of the world's most famous skyscrapers.

The main attraction for many visitors is the observation decks on the 86th and 102nd floors. The 86th-floor observatory, accessible via high-speed elevators, offers an open-air deck with panoramic views of New York City and beyond. From here, visitors can see landmarks such as Central Park, the Brooklyn Bridge, and the Statue of Liberty, with visibility extending up to 80 miles on a clear day. The 102nd-floor observatory, enclosed with floor-to-ceiling windows, provides an even higher vantage point for breathtaking views of the city.

In addition to the observation decks, the Empire State Building offers several exhibits that delve into its history, construction, and cultural significance. The Dare to Dream exhibit on the 80th floor showcases original documents, photographs, and architectural sketches, providing an in-depth look at the building's conception and construction. Another highlight is the Sustainability Exhibit, which details the building's recent energy-efficient retrofits, making it a model of sustainability.

The Empire State Building is also famous for its nightly illuminations, which light up the skyline with vibrant colors to celebrate holidays, events, and causes. These light displays have become a beloved feature of the city, adding to the building's allure and significance.

A visit to the Empire State Building is a quintessential New York experience, offering a unique blend of history, architecture, and breathtaking views. It continues to inspire awe and admiration, standing as a beacon of the city's resilience and innovation.

Times Square

Times Square, often referred to as "The Crossroads of the World," is one of the most vibrant and bustling areas in New York City. Located at the intersection of Broadway and Seventh Avenue, this iconic commercial and entertainment hub draws millions of visitors each year with its dazzling lights, towering billboards, and lively atmosphere.

Times Square's history dates back to the early 20th century when it became the heart of the theater district. Named after The New York Times moved its headquarters to the area in 1904, the square quickly evolved into a bustling center of entertainment and commerce. Today, it remains a focal point for Broadway theaters, restaurants, shops, and cultural events.

One of the most striking features of Times Square is its array of electronic billboards and neon signs. These vibrant displays, some of the largest in the world, create a kaleidoscope of colors and lights that illuminate the area day and night. The iconic New Year's Eve ball drop, held annually in Times Square, is watched by millions of people around the globe, marking the square as a symbol of celebration and unity.

Visitors to Times Square can enjoy a variety of activities and attractions. The area is home to numerous Broadway theaters, where world-famous musicals and plays are performed nightly. The TKTS booth, located beneath the red steps in Duffy Square, offers discounted tickets to many of these shows, making it a popular spot for theater enthusiasts.

In addition to Broadway, Times Square boasts a wide range of dining options, from fast food to fine dining. Renowned restaurants like Carmine's and The Capital Grille provide memorable dining experiences, while numerous street vendors offer quick bites for those on the go.

Times Square is also a shopping destination, with flagship stores like the Disney Store, M&M's World, and the Hard Rock Cafe attracting tourists and locals alike. Street performers, costumed characters, and live entertainment further enhance the lively atmosphere, creating a unique and unforgettable experience for visitors.

Cultural attractions in the area include the Times Square Museum and Visitor Center, which offers historical exhibits and information about the square's evolution. Nearby, the Museum of Modern Art (MoMA) and the New York Public Library provide additional cultural enrichment.

Times Square is not just a place; it's an experience. Its energy, excitement, and iconic status make it a must-visit destination for anyone exploring New York City, capturing the essence of the city's dynamic spirit and endless possibilities.

Central Park

Central Park, an urban oasis nestled in the heart of Manhattan, spans 843 acres and offers a tranquil retreat from the city's hustle and bustle. Designed by Frederick Law Olmsted and Calvert Vaux, this iconic park has been a centerpiece of New York City since its opening in 1858. It is the most visited urban park in the United States, attracting millions of visitors each year with its natural beauty, recreational activities, and cultural landmarks.

One of the park's most famous features is the Great Lawn, a vast open space perfect for picnics, sunbathing, and sports. Nearby, the Central Park Zoo and the Tisch Children's Zoo offer interactive experiences with animals from around the world, delighting visitors of all ages. The park also houses the Central Park Conservatory Garden, a meticulously maintained six-acre garden with themed sections that showcase seasonal flowers and lush greenery.

For those seeking outdoor recreation, Central Park boasts numerous trails for walking, running, and cycling. The 6.1-mile loop around the park is a favorite route for joggers and bikers, while the peaceful paths through the Ramble provide a more secluded experience. Boating on the Central Park Lake, especially in a rented rowboat or a gondola, offers a unique perspective of the park's serene landscapes.

Cultural attractions within Central Park include the Bethesda Terrace and Fountain, known for its stunning architecture and central location. The terrace's intricate tile work and grand staircase provide a picturesque setting for photos and gatherings. Nearby, the Loeb Boathouse offers dining with a view, as well as boat rentals and gondola rides.

The park is also home to numerous sculptures and monuments, including the iconic Alice in Wonderland statue and the literary-inspired

Shakespeare Garden. The Delacorte Theater hosts the annual Shakespeare in the Park festival, offering free performances of classic plays to the public.

Central Park is more than just a green space; it is a vibrant cultural hub that reflects the diverse spirit of New York City. Whether you are exploring its winding trails, attending a summer concert, or simply enjoying the tranquility of nature, Central Park offers an unforgettable experience for both locals and visitors.

Brooklyn Bridge

The Brooklyn Bridge, an architectural marvel and a symbol of New York City, spans the East River and connects the boroughs of Manhattan and Brooklyn. Completed in 1883, the bridge was the world's longest suspension bridge at the time and remains one of the most iconic and photographed landmarks in the city. Designed by John Augustus Roebling and completed by his son, Washington Roebling, after John's untimely death, the bridge stands as a testament to engineering ingenuity and human perseverance.

Walking or biking across the Brooklyn Bridge is a quintessential New York experience, offering stunning views of the city skyline, the Statue of Liberty, and the East River. The pedestrian walkway, elevated above the vehicle lanes, provides a safe and scenic route for travelers. The bridge's distinctive Gothic-style towers and web of steel cables create a dramatic backdrop for photographs and a sense of awe as you traverse its span.

The Brooklyn Bridge's significance extends beyond its architectural and engineering feats. It has played a vital role in the city's development, facilitating commerce and communication between Manhattan and Brooklyn. The bridge's completion was a major event, celebrated with fireworks and attended by thousands of New Yorkers, marking the beginning of a new era of urban connectivity.

The bridge's construction was not without challenges. Washington Roebling suffered from caisson disease (decompression sickness) due to working in the underwater chambers used to lay the foundations. Despite his illness, he continued to oversee the project from his home, with his wife, Emily Warren Roebling, playing a crucial role in communicating his instructions to the construction team. Emily's involvement was pivotal, and she became a respected figure in the engineering community.

Today, the Brooklyn Bridge remains a vital artery for traffic and a beloved landmark for New Yorkers and tourists alike. Its presence is a reminder of the city's rich history and its ability to overcome obstacles through innovation and determination. Whether viewed from the Brooklyn Heights Promenade, Dumbo, or the shores of Manhattan, the Brooklyn Bridge stands as a symbol of New York City's enduring spirit and its continuous quest for progress and connection.

Rockefeller Center

Rockefeller Center, located in the heart of Midtown Manhattan, is an iconic complex known for its Art Deco architecture, entertainment venues, and vibrant public spaces. Developed by John D. Rockefeller Jr. during the Great Depression, it stands as a symbol of American resilience and ingenuity. The complex comprises 19 commercial buildings spread over 22 acres, making it a bustling hub of activity for both locals and tourists.

One of the center's most famous features is the Rockefeller Plaza, home to the annual Christmas tree lighting ceremony and the ice skating rink. The tradition of the Christmas tree, which began in 1933, has become a beloved holiday event, drawing crowds from around the world. The ice rink, open from October to April, provides a picturesque setting for skating amidst the towering buildings.

The Top of the Rock Observation Deck offers breathtaking panoramic views of New York City. Located on the 70th floor of the GE Building (30 Rockefeller Plaza), it provides unobstructed vistas of Central Park, the Empire State Building, and the city's sprawling skyline. The observation deck's unique multi-level design and transparent safety barriers enhance the viewing experience, making it a must-visit for photographers and sightseers.

Rockefeller Center is also home to NBC Studios, where popular shows like "Saturday Night Live," "The Tonight Show Starring Jimmy Fallon," and "Today" are filmed. Guided tours of the studios offer behind-the-scenes glimpses into the world of television production and the chance to see iconic sets and studios.

The complex boasts an impressive collection of public art and sculptures, including the famous "Atlas" statue and the "Prometheus" sculpture overlooking the skating rink. The Channel Gardens, adorned with seasonal floral displays and fountains, provide a tranquil escape amidst the urban hustle.

Shopping and dining options abound in Rockefeller Center, with a mix of high-end retailers, specialty shops, and diverse eateries. The concourse level, connected by an underground network of passageways, offers convenient access to various shops and restaurants, making it a popular destination for visitors and office workers alike.

Rockefeller Center's cultural and historical significance, combined with its modern attractions, make it a vibrant destination in New York City. Whether you're ice skating in the winter, enjoying the views from Top of the Rock, or exploring its art and architecture, Rockefeller Center offers a dynamic and unforgettable experience.

Chrysler Building

The Chrysler Building, an Art Deco masterpiece and an iconic symbol of New York City's skyline, stands at 1,046 feet tall in Midtown Manhattan. Completed in 1930, it was briefly the tallest building in the world until it was surpassed by the Empire State Building in 1931. Designed by architect William Van Alen for the Chrysler Corporation, the building is renowned for its distinctive and innovative design.

The Chrysler Building's most striking feature is its terraced crown, which consists of seven radiating arches clad in stainless steel. The crown is adorned with triangular windows and intricate detailing that glistens in the sunlight, creating a dazzling effect that can be seen from miles away. The building's spire, an unexpected addition during construction, was secretly assembled inside the structure and hoisted into place in a dramatic bid to outdo the completion of 40 Wall Street, making it the tallest structure of its time.

The building's exterior is decorated with automotive-inspired elements, reflecting the Chrysler Corporation's heritage. These include gargoyles modeled after Chrysler hood ornaments, hubcaps, and radiator caps, which add to the building's unique and futuristic appearance.

Inside, the lobby of the Chrysler Building is a marvel of Art Deco design, featuring polished marble walls, an ornate ceiling mural, and custom-designed elevators. The mural, painted by artist Edward Trumbull, depicts scenes of aviation and the Chrysler assembly line, celebrating the era's technological advancements.

Although the building primarily serves as office space and does not have an observation deck open to the public, its lobby remains accessible to visitors who wish to admire its architectural beauty. The Chrysler Building's iconic status has made it a favorite subject for photographers, filmmakers, and artists, solidifying its place in popular culture.

The Chrysler Building is not just a testament to architectural innovation but also a symbol of the ambition and creativity that defined New York City during the early 20th century. Its timeless elegance and distinctive design continue to captivate admirers, making it a beloved landmark in the ever-evolving skyline of Manhattan.

One World Trade Center (Freedom Tower)

One World Trade Center, also known as the Freedom Tower, stands as a powerful symbol of resilience and renewal in Lower Manhattan. Rising to a height of 1,776 feet, it is the tallest building in the Western Hemisphere and the centerpiece of the rebuilt World Trade Center complex. Completed in 2013, One World Trade Center is a testament to the strength and determination of New York City and the nation in the aftermath of the September 11, 2001, terrorist attacks.

Designed by architect David Childs of Skidmore, Owings & Merrill, the tower's design integrates innovative engineering and sustainable practices. Its striking appearance features a shimmering glass façade that reflects the sky, creating a visual connection between the earth and the heavens. The building's height of 1,776 feet was chosen to symbolize the year of American independence, further emphasizing its role as a beacon of hope and resilience.

Visitors to One World Trade Center can experience the awe-inspiring views from the One World Observatory, located on the 100th, 101st, and 102nd floors. The journey to the observatory begins with a high-speed elevator ride, during which immersive displays showcase the development of New York City's skyline over centuries. Upon reaching the top, the observatory offers breathtaking 360-degree views of the city, the Hudson River, and beyond, providing a perspective that is both humbling and exhilarating.

The observatory experience includes several interactive exhibits and features, such as the Sky Portal, a circular glass floor that provides a thrilling view of the streets below. The "See Forever Theater" presents a short film that captures the energy and spirit of New York City, further enhancing the visit.

One World Trade Center is also notable for its advanced safety and sustainability features. The building incorporates a high-strength concrete core, state-of-the-art fireproofing, and energy-efficient systems, setting new standards for skyscraper design.

At its base, the National September 11 Memorial & Museum honors the nearly 3,000 victims of the 2001 attacks and the 1993 World Trade Center bombing. The twin reflecting pools, surrounded by the names of those who perished, offer a place of reflection and remembrance.

One World Trade Center stands not only as a remarkable architectural achievement but also as a poignant reminder of the strength, resilience, and unity of New York City and the nation. It is a must-visit destination for those seeking to understand the profound impact of the events of 9/11 and to appreciate the city's indomitable spirit.

Fifth Avenue

Fifth Avenue, one of the most famous streets in the world, stretches through the heart of Manhattan, offering a vibrant blend of luxury shopping, historic landmarks, and cultural institutions. Known as "Millionaire's Row" during the Gilded Age, Fifth Avenue has evolved into an iconic symbol of New York City's opulence and grandeur.

Starting at Washington Square Park in Greenwich Village and extending north to 143rd Street in Harlem, Fifth Avenue passes through some of Manhattan's most renowned neighborhoods and attractions. The avenue's most glamorous stretch, from 34th to 59th Streets, is home to high-end retailers, flagship stores, and world-famous department stores. Luxury brands like Tiffany & Co., Cartier, and Louis Vuitton line the avenue, attracting shoppers from around the globe seeking the latest in fashion and accessories.

In addition to its retail allure, Fifth Avenue is rich in cultural and architectural landmarks. One of the most notable is the New York Public Library's Stephen A. Schwarzman Building, located at 42nd Street. This Beaux-Arts masterpiece, flanked by its iconic lion statues, offers visitors a chance to explore its grand reading rooms, special exhibitions, and extensive collections.

Another architectural gem is St. Patrick's Cathedral, situated between 50th and 51st Streets. This stunning Gothic Revival structure, with its soaring spires and intricate stained-glass windows, serves as a serene counterpoint to the bustling commercial activity outside. It is a place of worship and reflection for millions of visitors and locals each year.

Fifth Avenue is also home to several world-class museums, collectively known as Museum Mile, stretching from 82nd to 105th Streets. The Metropolitan Museum of Art, one of the largest and most prestigious art museums in the world, anchors this cultural corridor. Other notable institutions include the Solomon R. Guggenheim Museum, renowned for its distinctive spiral design by Frank Lloyd Wright, and the Cooper Hewitt, Smithsonian Design Museum.

During the holiday season, Fifth Avenue transforms into a festive wonderland with elaborate window displays and the famous Rockefeller Center Christmas tree. The Saks Fifth Avenue light show, set to music, draws crowds of spectators who marvel at the dazzling display of lights and creativity.

Whether you are indulging in a shopping spree, admiring architectural landmarks, or exploring world-class museums, Fifth Avenue offers an unparalleled experience that captures the essence of New York City's vibrancy and sophistication. It remains a must-visit destination for anyone seeking to immerse themselves in the grandeur and cultural richness of the city.

Grand Central Terminal

Grand Central Terminal, often simply referred to as Grand Central, is one of New York City's most iconic landmarks and a masterpiece of Beaux-Arts architecture. Located at 42nd Street and Park Avenue in Midtown Manhattan, the terminal serves as a major transportation hub, a historic site, and a bustling center of activity for both commuters and tourists.

Completed in 1913, Grand Central Terminal was designed by the architectural firms Reed and Stem and Warren and Wetmore. Its grandiose design and intricate detailing reflect the opulence and ambition of the early 20th century. The terminal's main concourse, with its soaring 125-foot ceiling adorned with a celestial mural, is one of the most awe-inspiring public spaces in the city. The mural, painted by French artist Paul César Helleu, depicts a Mediterranean sky with constellations, and its restoration in the 1990s returned it to its original splendor.

Grand Central is more than just a transportation hub; it is a destination in itself. The terminal houses an array of shops, restaurants, and bars, offering a diverse range of dining and shopping experiences. The Grand Central Market, located on the east side of the terminal, features fresh produce, gourmet foods, and artisanal products, making it a favorite stop for food enthusiasts.

One of the terminal's most famous features is the opal-faced clock atop the information booth in the main concourse. This iconic clock is a popular meeting spot and a symbol of the terminal's timeless elegance. Another notable feature is the Whispering Gallery near the Oyster Bar, where the unique acoustics allow visitors to whisper into one corner and be heard clearly across the gallery.

Grand Central Terminal also boasts several fine dining options, including the historic Grand Central Oyster Bar & Restaurant, which has been serving fresh seafood since 1913. The terminal's cocktail lounges and bars, such as the Campbell Bar, offer sophisticated settings for enjoying a drink in a historic ambiance.

The terminal's extensive network of tracks and platforms serves the Metro-North Railroad, providing commuter rail service to the northern suburbs of New York City, including Westchester, Putnam, and Dutchess counties, as well as parts of Connecticut. The terminal's strategic location and connectivity make it a vital link in the region's transportation system.

Grand Central Terminal's historical and architectural significance, combined with its vibrant atmosphere and array of amenities, make it a must-visit destination for anyone exploring New York City. Whether you are catching a train, dining in style, or simply marveling at the grandeur of the terminal, Grand Central offers a unique and unforgettable experience that captures the essence of the city's rich history and dynamic energy.

Bryant Park

Bryant Park, a vibrant green oasis nestled in the heart of Midtown Manhattan, is a cherished destination for both locals and tourists. Spanning nearly 10 acres, the park offers a tranquil escape amidst the bustling city, surrounded by some of New York's most iconic skyscrapers, including the New York Public Library's main branch.

Established in 1847 and revitalized in the 1990s, Bryant Park has become one of New York City's most beloved public spaces. Its central lawn, meticulously maintained and open for lounging during warmer months, is a popular spot for picnics, sunbathing, and casual gatherings. The park's shaded pathways, bordered by lush gardens, are perfect for leisurely strolls, offering a picturesque setting that contrasts beautifully with the surrounding urban landscape.

Bryant Park is not just a place for relaxation; it's a hub of activity year-round. During the summer, the park hosts free outdoor movie nights, where visitors can enjoy classic films under the stars. Other events include yoga classes, live performances, and the beloved winter market, known as the Bank of America Winter Village, which features an ice skating rink and numerous holiday shops. This transformation into a winter wonderland makes Bryant Park a must-visit during the holiday season.

The park is also home to several eateries and cafes, where visitors can enjoy a meal or a coffee while taking in the vibrant atmosphere. The outdoor seating areas provide the perfect spot to people-watch or simply unwind.

Bryant Park's blend of natural beauty, cultural events, and convenient location makes it a unique and essential part of any New York City itinerary. Whether you're seeking relaxation, entertainment, or a picturesque backdrop, Bryant Park offers something for everyone in the heart of the city.

Museums and Cultural Institutions

The Metropolitan Museum of Art

The Metropolitan Museum of Art, commonly known as "The Met," is one of the largest and most prestigious art museums in the world. Located on the eastern edge of Central Park along Fifth Avenue, The Met spans over two million square feet and houses more than two million works of art, representing 5,000 years of human history. Established in 1870, the museum's mission is to collect, preserve, study, exhibit, and encourage appreciation for art.

The Met's vast and diverse collection is organized into 17 curatorial departments, each offering a comprehensive view of art from different cultures and periods. The Egyptian Art collection, for example, features the famous Temple of Dendur, a reconstructed ancient temple transported from Egypt, and a vast array of artifacts, including statues, jewelry, and mummies. The European Paintings department boasts masterpieces by artists such as Rembrandt, Vermeer, Van Gogh, and Monet, offering visitors a chance to view some of the most celebrated works in art history.

The museum's Arms and Armor collection is another highlight, showcasing an extensive array of weaponry and armor from various cultures and periods. The American Wing, meanwhile, provides a deep dive into American art and history, featuring colonial and early federal period rooms, as well as iconic paintings and sculptures by artists like John Singer Sargent and Frederic Edwin Church.

The Met is also renowned for its special exhibitions, which often draw record crowds. These exhibitions range from thematic surveys of specific periods or movements to in-depth retrospectives of individual artists. In addition to its exhibitions, The Met offers a variety of educational programs, including lectures, tours, and workshops, designed to engage and inspire visitors of all ages.

The museum's main building on Fifth Avenue is a work of art in itself, featuring impressive Beaux-Arts architecture and a grand entrance that sets the tone for the treasures within. The Met Cloisters, located in Fort Tryon Park in Upper Manhattan, is a branch of the museum dedicated to the art and architecture of medieval Europe, housed in a stunning building designed to evoke a medieval monastery.

A visit to The Metropolitan Museum of Art is a journey through time and across cultures, offering an unparalleled opportunity to explore the richness and diversity of human creativity. Whether you are an art enthusiast or a casual visitor, The Met provides a deeply enriching and unforgettable experience.

Museum of Modern Art (MoMA)

The Museum of Modern Art (MoMA), located in Midtown Manhattan, is one of the world's foremost institutions dedicated to contemporary and modern art. Since its founding in 1929, MoMA has played a pivotal role in the development and appreciation of modern art, offering an extensive collection that spans painting, sculpture, photography, film, design, and performance art.

MoMA's collection includes some of the most iconic works of the 20th and 21st centuries, representing a wide range of artistic movements and styles. Among its most famous pieces are Vincent van Gogh's "The Starry Night," Salvador Dalí's "The Persistence of Memory," and Pablo Picasso's "Les Demoiselles d'Avignon." These masterpieces, along with works by artists such as Henri Matisse, Jackson Pollock, Andy Warhol, and Frida Kahlo, highlight the museum's commitment to showcasing groundbreaking and influential art.

In addition to its permanent collection, MoMA is renowned for its dynamic and innovative exhibitions. These exhibitions often explore specific themes, artists, or movements, providing visitors with fresh perspectives and deeper insights into modern and contemporary art. The museum's curatorial approach emphasizes both historical context and contemporary relevance, making each exhibition a thought-provoking experience.

MoMA's architecture, redesigned by Yoshio Taniguchi and expanded by Diller Scofidio + Renfro, reflects its modernist ethos. The sleek, minimalist design of the building creates an inviting and open environment, allowing the art to take center stage. The museum's Sculpture Garden, an outdoor oasis featuring works by artists such as Alexander Calder and Auguste Rodin, offers a tranquil space for reflection amidst the bustling city.

The museum also hosts a variety of educational programs and events, including lectures, film screenings, and workshops. These programs aim to engage audiences of all ages and backgrounds, fostering a deeper understanding and appreciation of modern art. MoMA's film department, in particular, is highly regarded, presenting an eclectic mix of classic and contemporary cinema from around the world.

MoMA's impact extends beyond its walls through its digital initiatives and publications, which make its collection and scholarship accessible to a global audience. Whether visiting in person or exploring online, the Museum of Modern Art offers an enriching and inspiring experience, showcasing the transformative power of modern and contemporary art.

American Museum of Natural History

The American Museum of Natural History (AMNH), located on the Upper West Side of Manhattan, is one of the world's preeminent institutions dedicated to the exploration and understanding of the natural world. Founded in 1869, the museum spans 26 interconnected buildings and houses over 34 million specimens and artifacts, making it one of the largest and most comprehensive natural history museums globally.

The museum's vast collection covers a wide range of scientific disciplines, including anthropology, paleontology, zoology, geology, and astronomy. One of the museum's most famous exhibits is the Hall of Saurischian Dinosaurs, which features the awe-inspiring Tyrannosaurus rex and the towering Barosaurus. The museum's dinosaur collection is among the most extensive in the world, attracting millions of visitors each year.

Another highlight is the Rose Center for Earth and Space, which includes the Hayden Planetarium. This state-of-the-art facility, designed by James Stewart Polshek, features a giant sphere that houses the Space Theater, where visitors can experience immersive shows about the universe, narrated by renowned astrophysicists like Neil deGrasse Tyson. The Hall of the Universe and the Hall of Planet Earth offer interactive exhibits that explore the cosmos and our planet's geological processes.

The AMNH is also home to the Hall of Biodiversity, which showcases the variety and interconnectedness of life on Earth. This exhibit features a breathtaking diorama of a rainforest, highlighting the rich diversity of species and the importance of conservation. The Hall of Ocean Life, with its iconic 94-foot-long model of a blue whale suspended from the ceiling, provides a fascinating look at marine ecosystems.

Cultural and anthropological exhibits at the museum offer insights into human history and cultures from around the world. The Hall of African Peoples, the Hall of Asian Peoples, and the Hall of Pacific Peoples display artifacts, tools, and art from various civilizations, illustrating the diversity and ingenuity of human societies.

In addition to its permanent exhibits, the AMNH hosts temporary exhibitions that delve into specific scientific topics and discoveries. The museum's educational programs, including workshops, lectures, and special events, aim to engage and inspire learners of all ages.

The American Museum of Natural History is more than just a museum; it is a center for scientific research and education. With its extensive collections, innovative exhibits, and commitment to discovery, the AMNH offers a captivating journey through the wonders of the natural world and human history. Whether you are a science enthusiast or a curious visitor, the museum provides an enriching and unforgettable experience.

Guggenheim Museum

The Solomon R. Guggenheim Museum, commonly known as the Guggenheim, is an iconic art museum located on the Upper East Side of Manhattan. Designed by the renowned architect Frank Lloyd Wright, the museum's distinctive cylindrical building, which opened in 1959, is considered one of the most significant architectural landmarks of the 20th century. Its unique design features a spiraling ramp gallery that ascends from the ground level to the top of the building, providing a continuous and fluid viewing experience.

The Guggenheim Museum houses an impressive collection of modern and contemporary art, encompassing works from the late 19th century to the present day. The collection includes masterpieces by pioneering artists such as Wassily Kandinsky, Paul Klee, Piet Mondrian, and Pablo Picasso. The museum's holdings are particularly strong in abstract and non-objective art, reflecting the vision of its founder, Solomon R. Guggenheim, and his advisor, artist Hilla Rebay.

In addition to its permanent collection, the Guggenheim is known for its innovative and thought-provoking temporary exhibitions. These exhibitions often explore specific themes, artists, or movements, providing visitors with fresh perspectives on modern and contemporary art. The museum's curatorial approach emphasizes interdisciplinary connections, bringing together visual art, architecture, design, and performance.

One of the highlights of visiting the Guggenheim is the experience of navigating Wright's iconic spiral ramp. As visitors ascend the ramp, they encounter artworks in a chronological sequence, allowing for a unique and immersive journey through the history of modern art. The skylight at the top of the rotunda bathes the space in natural light, enhancing the viewing experience.

The Guggenheim also offers a range of educational programs and public events, including lectures, film screenings, and workshops. These programs aim to engage and inspire audiences of all ages, fostering a deeper understanding and appreciation of modern and contemporary art.

The Guggenheim Museum's architectural brilliance, coupled with its exceptional art collection and dynamic exhibitions, makes it a must-visit destination for art enthusiasts and tourists alike. It stands as a testament to the transformative power of art and architecture, providing an unforgettable experience for all who visit.

Whitney Museum of American Art

The Whitney Museum of American Art, located in the Meatpacking District of Manhattan, is a premier institution dedicated to the art of the United States. Founded in 1930 by Gertrude Vanderbilt Whitney, a prominent sculptor and art patron, the museum has a longstanding commitment to supporting contemporary American artists. The Whitney's mission is to collect, preserve, interpret, and exhibit American art, with a focus on works from the 20th and 21st centuries.

The Whitney's collection encompasses over 25,000 works of art, including paintings, sculptures, photographs, films, and new media. It features iconic pieces by influential American artists such as Edward Hopper, Georgia O'Keeffe, Alexander Calder, and Jackson Pollock. The museum is particularly renowned for its holdings of works by artists associated with the Ashcan School, Abstract Expressionism, and Pop Art, offering a comprehensive overview of American art movements.

In 2015, the Whitney moved to its current location in a striking building designed by architect Renzo Piano. Situated at the southern end of the High Line, the museum's new home provides expansive gallery spaces, state-of-the-art facilities, and breathtaking views of the Hudson River and the city skyline. The building's design emphasizes transparency and accessibility, with large windows and outdoor terraces that invite visitors to engage with both the art and the surrounding urban environment.

One of the Whitney's signature events is the Whitney Biennial, a landmark exhibition that has taken place since 1932. The Biennial showcases the latest developments in American art, featuring works by emerging and established artists. It is a key platform for contemporary artists to present their work and for audiences to experience the evolving landscape of American art.

In addition to its exhibitions, the Whitney offers a robust schedule of educational programs, public events, and performances. These include artist talks, panel discussions, film screenings, and family-friendly activities, all designed to engage diverse audiences and foster a deeper appreciation of contemporary art.

The Whitney Museum of American Art is a vibrant and dynamic institution that plays a crucial role in the cultural life of New York City. Its commitment to showcasing innovative and thought-provoking works of art makes it a must-visit destination for art lovers and anyone interested in the rich and diverse tapestry of American art.

The Frick Collection

The Frick Collection, housed in the elegant mansion of industrialist Henry Clay Frick on Manhattan's Upper East Side, is one of New York City's most esteemed art museums. Established in 1935, the museum offers an intimate and refined setting to view an exceptional collection of European paintings, sculpture, and decorative arts. The collection reflects Frick's discerning taste and passion for art, amassed during his lifetime and bequeathed to the public.

The Frick Collection is renowned for its masterpieces by some of the most celebrated artists of the Western canon. The collection includes works by Titian, Rembrandt, Vermeer, Goya, and Gainsborough, among others. Highlights include Johannes Vermeer's "Mistress and Maid," Rembrandt's "Self-Portrait," and James McNeill Whistler's "Arrangement in Black and Gold." The museum's holdings also feature fine examples of French furniture, Italian Renaissance bronzes, and Limoges enamels.

The mansion itself, designed by architect Thomas Hastings and completed in 1914, is a masterpiece of Beaux-Arts architecture. The interior spaces, including the Oval Room, the West Gallery, and the Garden Court, are meticulously designed to complement the artworks they house. The mansion's opulent yet welcoming atmosphere provides a unique and personal experience, allowing visitors to appreciate the art in a setting reminiscent of a grand private home.

In addition to its permanent collection, The Frick hosts temporary exhibitions that delve into specific aspects of its holdings or present works on loan from other institutions. These exhibitions often provide new insights into well-known works or introduce visitors to lesser-known artists and art forms. The museum also offers a variety of educational programs, including lectures, symposia, and guided tours, designed to deepen the public's understanding and appreciation of its collection.

One of the most beloved features of The Frick Collection is its tranquil garden courtyard, a serene space filled with lush greenery, classical sculptures, and a central fountain. This oasis offers a peaceful retreat from the bustling city and enhances the overall visitor experience.

The Frick Collection's commitment to preserving and presenting high-quality art in an intimate and elegant setting makes it a treasured cultural institution. Its unique blend of art, architecture, and history provides a deeply enriching experience for all who visit, ensuring its status as a must-see destination in New York City.

New-York Historical Society

The New-York Historical Society, established in 1804, is the oldest museum in New York City and a preeminent institution dedicated to the history of the United States and New York. Located on Central Park West at 77th Street, the museum offers a comprehensive view of the city's and nation's past through its extensive collections, exhibitions, and educational programs.

The museum's collection includes more than 1.6 million works, encompassing a wide range of artifacts, artworks, documents, and historical objects. Highlights include an extensive collection of American paintings, sculptures, and decorative arts, as well as an impressive archive of photographs, manuscripts, and rare books. The society's library holds an invaluable array of materials that are essential for researching American history.

One of the New-York Historical Society's most notable features is its immersive exhibitions that bring history to life. These exhibitions cover a broad spectrum of topics, from the founding of New York City to pivotal moments in American history, such as the Revolutionary War, the Civil

War, and the civil rights movement. The museum also hosts temporary exhibitions that delve into specific historical themes or figures, often featuring rare artifacts and engaging multimedia displays.

In addition to its exhibitions, the New-York Historical Society offers a variety of educational programs designed to engage audiences of all ages. These include lectures, panel discussions, and workshops that explore historical topics in depth. The museum's family programs, such as storytime sessions and interactive tours, make history accessible and enjoyable for younger visitors.

The society also houses the DiMenna Children's History Museum, a dedicated space where children can learn about history through hands-on activities and interactive exhibits. This museum within a museum offers an engaging and educational experience that fosters a lifelong interest in history.

The New-York Historical Society's mission is to illuminate the rich and complex history of New York and the United States, providing context and insight into the events and people that have shaped the nation. Its comprehensive collections, dynamic exhibitions, and diverse educational programs make it an essential destination for anyone interested in American history and culture.

Museum of the City of New York

The Museum of the City of New York, located at the top of Museum Mile on Fifth Avenue and 103rd Street, is a vital institution dedicated to preserving and presenting the history and culture of New York City. Founded in 1923, the museum offers a rich tapestry of exhibitions, collections, and programs that capture the spirit and evolution of the city.

The museum's collection comprises over 750,000 objects, including photographs, maps, manuscripts, costumes, and decorative arts. These artifacts provide a comprehensive and vivid portrayal of New York City's development from its early days as a Dutch settlement to its present status as a global metropolis. Key highlights include the museum's extensive photography collection, which documents the city's dynamic changes and diverse populations, and its holdings of theatrical memorabilia, reflecting New York's pivotal role in the world of entertainment.

One of the museum's standout features is its permanent exhibition, "New York at Its Core," which explores the city's 400-year history through immersive displays, multimedia installations, and interactive elements. The exhibition is divided into three galleries: "Port City" (1609-1898), "World City" (1898-2012), and "Future City Lab," which invites visitors to consider the future challenges and opportunities facing New York.

In addition to its permanent exhibition, the Museum of the City of New York hosts a variety of temporary exhibitions that delve into specific aspects of the city's history and culture. These exhibitions often highlight underrepresented communities and untold stories, offering fresh perspectives on New York's multifaceted identity.

The museum's educational programs and public events are designed to engage a broad audience, from schoolchildren to adults. Programs include guided tours, lectures, panel discussions, and workshops that explore topics such as urban planning, social justice, and cultural heritage. The museum also offers family-friendly activities, making it an accessible and enriching destination for visitors of all ages.

The Museum of the City of New York is housed in a beautiful Georgian Revival building, which provides an elegant and fitting backdrop for its collections and exhibitions. The museum's setting, combined with its comprehensive exploration of New York's history, makes it a must-visit destination for anyone seeking to understand the complexities and wonders of this remarkable city.

Intrepid Sea, Air & Space Museum

The Intrepid Sea, Air & Space Museum, located at Pier 86 on the Hudson River in Manhattan, is a unique institution dedicated to the exploration of history, science, and service through the lens of sea, air, and space innovation. Housed aboard the USS Intrepid, an aircraft carrier that served during World War II and the Vietnam War, the museum offers an immersive and educational experience that appeals to visitors of all ages.

The museum's centerpiece is the USS Intrepid itself, a National Historic Landmark that played a crucial role in American military history. Visitors can explore the ship's flight deck, hangar deck, and various exhibits that showcase the life and work of the sailors who served aboard. The Intrepid's impressive collection of aircraft, including fighter jets, helicopters, and reconnaissance planes, highlights the technological advancements and strategic importance of aviation in military operations.

In addition to the USS Intrepid, the museum features several other significant exhibits. The Space Shuttle Pavilion houses the space shuttle Enterprise, the prototype NASA orbiter that paved the way for the space shuttle program. The pavilion offers interactive exhibits and multimedia presentations that explore the history of space exploration and the technological innovations that made it possible.

The museum's submarine Growler, the only American guided missile submarine open to the public, provides a rare glimpse into the life of submariners during the Cold War. Visitors can tour the submarine's control room, torpedo room, and living quarters, gaining insight into the challenges and experiences of life beneath the sea.

The Intrepid Sea, Air & Space Museum also offers a range of educational programs and public events, including hands-on activities, STEM-focused workshops, and special exhibitions. These programs are designed to inspire curiosity and foster a deeper understanding of science, technology, and history.

The museum's location on the Hudson River provides a stunning backdrop for its exhibits, with panoramic views of Manhattan and the river adding to the overall experience. The Intrepid Sea, Air & Space Museum is not only a tribute to American innovation and bravery but also a dynamic educational institution that encourages exploration and discovery. It is a must-visit destination for anyone interested in the intersection of history, science, and technology.

The Morgan Library & Museum

The Morgan Library & Museum, located in the heart of New York City on Madison Avenue and 36th Street, is a world-renowned institution dedicated to the art of the book and the history of literature. Founded by the financier J.P. Morgan in 1906, the library began as a private collection and has since evolved into a public institution that houses an extraordinary collection of manuscripts, rare books, drawings, and prints.

The Morgan Library & Museum's collection includes some of the most significant literary and historical artifacts in the world. Highlights include original manuscripts by literary giants such as Charles Dickens, Jane Austen, and Mark Twain, as well as illuminated manuscripts, ancient texts, and rare printed books. The collection also features notable musical scores, including works by Mozart, Beethoven, and Chopin, providing a rich tapestry of cultural and intellectual history.

One of the museum's most captivating features is the Morgan's original library, a stunning Renaissance-style room designed by architect Charles McKim. The library's ornate interiors, filled with richly carved woodwork, frescoes, and a magnificent collection of rare books, offer a glimpse into the opulent world of J.P. Morgan. The adjoining rotunda, with its intricate mosaics and decorative arts, adds to the sense of grandeur and historical significance.

In addition to its permanent collection, the Morgan Library & Museum hosts a variety of temporary exhibitions that explore different aspects of its holdings and the broader world of art and literature. These exhibitions often include loans from other prestigious institutions and private collections, providing visitors with a unique and comprehensive viewing experience.

he museum also offers a range of educational programs, public lectures, and special events designed to engage and inspire visitors of all ages. These programs include literary readings, scholarly lectures, and interactive workshops that delve into the themes and stories behind the museum's collections.

The Morgan Library & Museum's commitment to preserving and presenting the art of the book, combined with its stunning architectural setting, makes it a cherished cultural institution in New York City. Whether you are a literature enthusiast, a history buff, or simply someone who appreciates the beauty of fine art and rare books, the Morgan Library & Museum offers an enriching and unforgettable experience.

Theaters and Performances

Broadway Theaters (collective)

Broadway Theaters, collectively known as "Broadway," form the epicenter of American theater and are synonymous with world-class performances and vibrant entertainment. Located in the Theater District of Midtown Manhattan, stretching from West 41st to West 54th Streets and from Sixth Avenue to Eighth Avenue, Broadway is home to 41 professional theaters, each with a seating capacity of 500 or more. The sheer concentration of theaters in this area creates a bustling cultural hub that attracts millions of theatergoers annually.

Broadway's history dates back to the early 19th century, but it truly flourished in the early 20th century with the advent of musical theater. Iconic theaters like the Majestic, the Shubert, and the Winter Garden have hosted countless legendary productions, from "Oklahoma!" and "West Side Story" to contemporary hits like "The Lion King," "Hamilton," and "Wicked." Broadway's influence extends far beyond its geographic boundaries, shaping the cultural landscape of America and the world.

Attending a Broadway show is a quintessential New York experience. Each theater offers a unique ambiance and history, contributing to the overall allure of Broadway. The productions range from lavish musicals and gripping dramas to innovative revivals and groundbreaking new works. The diverse array of shows ensures that there is something for everyone, whether you're a fan of classic tales or cutting-edge performances.

Broadway is not just about the performances; it's also about the people. The district is filled with aspiring actors, directors, producers, and countless other professionals who bring these productions to life. The energy and passion of the theater community are palpable, adding to the magic of Broadway.

In addition to the performances, Broadway is renowned for its vibrant atmosphere. Times Square, located at the heart of the Theater District, is known for its dazzling neon lights and massive digital billboards promoting current shows. The area is also filled with restaurants, bars, and shops catering to theatergoers, making it a lively destination before and after shows.

Broadway Theaters collectively represent the pinnacle of live performance, where artistic excellence and entertainment converge. Whether you are a theater aficionado or a first-time visitor, the experience of seeing a Broadway show is unparalleled, offering a glimpse into the heart and soul of New York City's cultural heritage.

Radio City Music Hall

Radio City Music Hall, located in the heart of Rockefeller Center in Midtown Manhattan, is an iconic entertainment venue renowned for its stunning Art Deco architecture and legendary performances. Since its opening in 1932, it has been one of New York City's premier destinations for music, theater, and special events, earning the nickname "Showplace of the Nation."

Designed by architect Edward Durell Stone and interior designer Donald Deskey, Radio City Music Hall features a grand and opulent interior that reflects the glamour and sophistication of the Art Deco era. The theater's auditorium, with its sweeping arches, intricate murals, and luxurious seating, can accommodate over 6,000 spectators, making it one of the largest indoor theaters in the world. The Great Stage, with its innovative hydraulic system, allows for spectacular set changes and dynamic performances.

One of the most famous events held at Radio City Music Hall is the annual Christmas Spectacular starring the Radio City Rockettes. This beloved holiday tradition, which began in 1933, features the high-kicking precision dance troupe in a dazzling show that includes festive music, elaborate costumes, and breathtaking choreography. The Christmas Spectacular has become a must-see event for both locals and tourists, drawing audiences from around the world.

In addition to the Christmas Spectacular, Radio City Music Hall hosts a wide variety of performances throughout the year, including concerts, Broadway shows, comedy acts, and award ceremonies. The venue's impressive acoustics and state-of-the-art technology make it a favored location for top performers and events, including the Grammy Awards, Tony Awards, and the MTV Video Music Awards.

Radio City Music Hall also offers guided tours that provide an insider's look at the theater's rich history and architectural marvels. Visitors can explore the lavish interiors, learn about the venue's storied past, and even meet a Rockette.

Beyond its role as a performance venue, Radio City Music Hall is a cultural landmark that embodies the spirit of New York City. Its grand design, storied history, and commitment to excellence in entertainment make it a beloved institution. Whether attending a show or taking a tour, a visit to Radio City Music Hall offers a glimpse into the golden age of entertainment and the enduring magic of live performance.

Lincoln Center for the Performing Arts

Lincoln Center for the Performing Arts, located on Manhattan's Upper West Side, is a world-renowned cultural complex that serves as a beacon for music, dance, theater, and film. Spanning 16.3 acres, Lincoln Center is home to 11 resident organizations, including the New York Philharmonic, the Metropolitan Opera, the New York City Ballet, and the Juilliard School, making it one of the most significant cultural institutions in the world.

Conceived in the mid-20th century as part of a broader urban renewal project, Lincoln Center opened in the 1960s and has since become a cornerstone of New York City's artistic and cultural life. The center's iconic architecture, designed by renowned architects such as Wallace K. Harrison and Philip Johnson, includes landmark buildings like the Metropolitan Opera House, Avery Fisher Hall (now David Geffen Hall), and the David H. Koch Theater.

Lincoln Center's diverse programming caters to a wide range of artistic tastes and interests. The Metropolitan Opera presents world-class operatic productions, featuring leading singers, directors, and conductors. The New York Philharmonic, America's oldest symphony orchestra, offers an extensive repertoire of classical and contemporary music. The New York City Ballet is celebrated for its innovative choreography and exceptional performances, while the Juilliard School trains the next generation of artists in music, dance, and drama.

In addition to its resident organizations, Lincoln Center hosts numerous festivals, series, and special events throughout the year. The Lincoln Center Festival, the Mostly Mozart Festival, and Lincoln Center Out of Doors are just a few examples of the diverse and dynamic programming that attracts audiences from around the globe. The center's public spaces, including the iconic Revson Fountain and the Josie Robertson Plaza, provide a beautiful and inviting setting for outdoor performances and gatherings.

Lincoln Center is also committed to education and community engagement. Its educational programs, including lectures, workshops, and masterclasses, aim to inspire and cultivate a love for the arts among people of all ages. The Lincoln Center Institute for the Arts in Education offers innovative arts education programs that integrate the performing arts into the school curriculum.

Lincoln Center for the Performing Arts stands as a testament to the transformative power of the arts. Its unparalleled array of performances, educational initiatives, and cultural events make it a vibrant and essential part of New York City's cultural landscape. Whether attending a world-class performance or exploring the beautiful campus, a visit to Lincoln Center is an enriching and inspiring experience.

Carnegie Hall

Carnegie Hall, located at 881 Seventh Avenue in Manhattan, is one of the most prestigious concert venues in the world. Since its opening in 1891, the hall has been synonymous with musical excellence and has hosted countless legendary performances. The building was funded by the philanthropist Andrew Carnegie and designed by architect William Burnet Tuthill, featuring a distinctive Italian Renaissance-style façade.

The main performance space, Stern Auditorium/Perelman Stage, is renowned for its impeccable acoustics and elegant design. With a seating capacity of 2,804, the auditorium has welcomed the greatest names in classical music, including Tchaikovsky, who conducted at the hall's inaugural concert, as well as performers like Leonard Bernstein, Vladimir Horowitz, and Maria Callas. The hall's acoustics are often considered some of the best in the world, providing an intimate yet grand listening experience.

Carnegie Hall also houses two smaller venues: Zankel Hall and Weill Recital Hall. Zankel Hall, with a capacity of 599, offers a versatile space for a wide range of musical genres and performances, from classical and jazz to world music and contemporary works. Weill Recital Hall, seating 268, is perfect for chamber music, solo recitals, and educational events.

Beyond its storied history and architectural beauty, Carnegie Hall is a vibrant institution that actively engages with the community. Its robust education and outreach programs, including the Weill Music Institute, offer music education to people of all ages and backgrounds. These programs include workshops, masterclasses, and interactive performances designed to inspire and nurture a love for music.

Carnegie Hall's commitment to diversity in programming ensures that it remains relevant and inclusive. Each season features a blend of classical masterpieces, contemporary compositions, jazz, pop, and world music, appealing to a broad audience. The hall also commissions new works, supporting the creation of innovative and forward-thinking music.

Attending a performance at Carnegie Hall is more than just a concert; it is a cultural experience steeped in history and artistic excellence. Whether you are a music aficionado or a casual listener, a visit to Carnegie Hall offers a chance to witness world-class performances in one of the most revered concert halls globally, making it a must-visit destination in New York City.

The Public Theater

The Public Theater, located at 425 Lafayette Street in Manhattan's NoHo neighborhood, is a cornerstone of New York City's vibrant theater scene. Founded in 1954 by Joseph Papp, The Public has a storied history of producing innovative and groundbreaking works that challenge, entertain, and provoke audiences. The theater is housed in the historic Astor Library building, a landmark that adds to its cultural and architectural significance.

The Public Theater is known for its commitment to fostering new talent and providing a platform for diverse voices. It has been the birthplace of numerous critically acclaimed productions that have gone on to achieve global recognition. One of its most notable achievements is the development of the musical "Hamilton" by Lin-Manuel Miranda, which began at The Public before transferring to Broadway and becoming a worldwide phenomenon. Other significant works include "A Chorus Line," "Fun Home," and "Hair."

The theater operates several performance spaces, each offering a unique and intimate setting for its productions. The largest is the Newman Theater, which hosts many of The Public's major productions. Other spaces include the Anspacher Theater, the Martinson Theater, the Shiva Theater, and Joe's Pub, a cabaret-style venue known for its eclectic lineup of music, comedy, and spoken word performances.

The Public Theater is also home to Shakespeare in the Park, a beloved New York City tradition that offers free performances of Shakespearean plays in Central Park's Delacorte Theater. This initiative, which began in 1962, reflects The Public's mission to make theater accessible to all, regardless of socioeconomic status.

In addition to its productions, The Public Theater offers a range of educational and community programs. These include artist residencies, workshops, and initiatives aimed at engaging young people and underserved communities. The theater's Mobile Unit brings free Shakespeare performances to community centers, correctional facilities, and other non-traditional venues throughout the city.

The Public Theater's dedication to artistic excellence, social relevance, and community engagement has solidified its reputation as one of the leading cultural institutions in the United States. Whether you are attending a provocative new play, a star-studded musical, or a free performance in the park, a visit to The Public Theater promises an enriching and unforgettable experience.

Apollo Theater

The Apollo Theater, located at 253 West 125th Street in Harlem, is one of the most iconic and culturally significant venues in the United States. Since its opening in 1934, the Apollo has been a cornerstone of African American culture and a launching pad for some of the most legendary performers in music history. Its storied past and ongoing commitment to showcasing emerging talent make it a vital part of New York City's artistic heritage.

The Apollo Theater is renowned for its Amateur Night, a talent competition that has been a tradition since the theater's early days. Amateur Night has discovered and launched the careers of countless stars, including Ella Fitzgerald, James Brown, Stevie Wonder, and Lauryn Hill. The weekly event remains a beloved fixture, attracting aspiring performers from around the world and offering audiences an electrifying experience.

The theater's historic stage has hosted a who's who of musical legends, spanning genres from jazz and blues to soul, R&B, and hip-hop. Notable performers include Billie Holiday, Duke Ellington, Aretha Franklin, Michael Jackson, and Prince. The Apollo has also been a key venue for political and cultural events, serving as a gathering place for community activism and civil rights movements.

The Apollo Theater's architecture and interior design reflect its rich history. The venue features a distinctive marquee, elegant Art Deco details, and a vibrant, welcoming atmosphere. The theater's main auditorium, with its excellent acoustics and sightlines, provides an intimate setting for performances, ensuring that every seat feels close to the action.

In addition to its live performances, the Apollo Theater offers a variety of educational and community programs. These include masterclasses, panel discussions, and workshops designed to inspire and nurture the next generation of artists. The Apollo's Historic Tour provides visitors with an in-depth look at the theater's history, including behind-the-scenes access and fascinating anecdotes about the legends who have graced its stage.

The Apollo Theater's commitment to artistic excellence and cultural heritage has made it a symbol of Harlem's enduring influence and a beacon for artists and audiences alike. Whether you are attending a star-studded concert, cheering on hopefuls at Amateur Night, or exploring the theater's storied past, a visit to the Apollo offers an unforgettable glimpse into the heart and soul of American music and culture.

Beacon Theatre

The Beacon Theatre, located at 2124 Broadway on the Upper West Side of Manhattan, is a renowned concert hall and performance venue with a rich history and stunning Art Deco architecture. Opened in 1929, the Beacon was originally designed as a movie palace by architect Walter W. Ahlschlager. Its elegant design features intricate moldings, stunning murals, and a grand chandelier, creating an atmosphere of opulence and timeless beauty.

The Beacon Theatre is known for its excellent acoustics and intimate setting, making it a favorite venue for both performers and audiences. With a seating capacity of 2,894, it offers an up-close and personal experience while still accommodating a substantial audience. The theater's layout ensures that every seat has a great view and sound, enhancing the overall experience of attending a performance here.

Over the years, the Beacon Theatre has hosted a wide range of events, including concerts, comedy shows, and theatrical productions. It is particularly famous for its rock and pop concerts, having welcomed legendary musicians such as the Allman Brothers Band, the Rolling Stones, Bob Dylan, and Paul Simon. The Allman Brothers Band, in particular, has a long-standing association with the Beacon, having performed numerous residencies at the venue.

In addition to music, the Beacon Theatre is a popular venue for stand-up comedy, with top comedians like Jerry Seinfeld, Chris Rock, and Louis C.K. having graced its stage. The theater also hosts special events, film screenings, and television broadcasts, adding to its diverse repertoire.

The Beacon Theatre underwent a major renovation in 2006, which restored many of its original Art Deco features and updated its facilities to modern standards. This meticulous restoration has preserved the theater's historical charm while ensuring a comfortable and state-of-the-art experience for today's audiences.

The Beacon Theatre's combination of historical significance, architectural beauty, and top-notch acoustics make it a beloved institution in New York City's cultural landscape. Whether you're attending a rock concert, a comedy show, or a special event, a visit to the Beacon Theatre promises an unforgettable experience in one of the city's most iconic venues.

New Amsterdam Theatre

The New Amsterdam Theatre, located at 214 West 42nd Street in the heart of New York City's Theater District, is a historic Broadway theater known for its opulent Art Nouveau design and significant role in the history of American theater. Opened in 1903, the theater was designed by architects Herts & Tallant and was one of the first theaters to be built in what would become the famous Broadway district.

The New Amsterdam Theatre's design features lavish details, including intricate plasterwork, stained glass, and elaborate murals by artist Alphonse Mucha. The theater's grand interior reflects the Art Nouveau style, with flowing lines, floral motifs, and a sense of elegance and fantasy. The stunning architecture and decor make the New Amsterdam one of the most beautiful theaters in New York City.

In its early years, the New Amsterdam Theatre was home to the Ziegfeld Follies, a series of elaborate theatrical productions that became synonymous with Broadway's golden age. The Follies featured a mix of music, dance, and comedy, and helped to launch the careers of many legendary performers, including Fanny Brice and W.C. Fields.

After a period of decline and neglect, the New Amsterdam Theatre underwent a massive restoration in the 1990s, led by the Walt Disney Company. The restoration returned the theater to its former glory, preserving its historic features while updating its facilities for modern audiences. The theater reopened in 1997 with the premiere of Disney's "The Lion King," which became a Broadway sensation.

Today, the New Amsterdam Theatre continues to host Disney's acclaimed Broadway productions, including long-running hits like "Mary Poppins" and "Aladdin." The theater's partnership with Disney has helped to revitalize 42nd Street and cement its status as a premier destination for family-friendly entertainment.

The New Amsterdam Theatre offers guided tours that provide a behind-the-scenes look at its history, architecture, and the magic of its productions. Visitors can explore the theater's opulent interiors, learn about its storied past, and see how it continues to enchant audiences today.

A visit to the New Amsterdam Theatre is a journey into the heart of Broadway's history and a celebration of the enduring appeal of live theater. Whether attending a Disney musical or exploring its magnificent architecture, the New Amsterdam offers an unforgettable experience in one of Broadway's most iconic venues.

Gershwin Theatre

The Gershwin Theatre, located at 222 West 51st Street in the heart of Manhattan's Theater District, is one of Broadway's largest and most prominent theaters. Named in honor of legendary composer George Gershwin and his lyricist brother Ira Gershwin, the theater is a tribute to their immense contributions to American music and theater. The Gershwin Theatre is known for its modern design, excellent sightlines, and state-of-the-art facilities, making it a favored venue for large-scale productions.

Opened in 1972 as the Uris Theatre, the venue was renamed the Gershwin Theatre in 1983 to honor the Gershwin brothers' legacy. The theater's design, by architect Ralph Alswang, reflects a contemporary aesthetic with a spacious auditorium and sleek lines. With a seating capacity of 1,933, the Gershwin Theatre is one of the largest on Broadway, providing ample space for elaborate sets and special effects.

The Gershwin Theatre's current long-running production is the hit musical "Wicked," which has been playing to sold-out audiences since it opened in 2003. "Wicked," a prequel to "The Wizard of Oz," tells the untold story of the Wicked Witch of the West and Glinda the Good Witch, offering a fresh and captivating perspective on the beloved classic. The musical's stunning visuals, powerful performances, and memorable score have made it a Broadway sensation and a must-see for theatergoers.

In addition to its main stage productions, the Gershwin Theatre houses the American Theatre Hall of Fame in its lobby. This exhibit honors the greatest figures in American theater, including actors, playwrights, directors, and producers who have made significant contributions to the art form. The Hall of Fame features plaques and memorabilia that celebrate the achievements and legacies of these theater legends.

The Gershwin Theatre's combination of modern amenities, historical significance, and exceptional productions make it a cornerstone of Broadway's vibrant theater scene. Whether attending a performance of "Wicked" or exploring the American Theatre Hall of Fame, a visit to the Gershwin Theatre offers a thrilling and memorable experience in one of New York City's premier cultural institutions.

St. James Theatre

The St. James Theatre, located at 246 West 44th Street in Manhattan's Theater District, is one of Broadway's most storied and beloved venues. Opened in 1927, the theater was designed by architect Warren and Wetmore, who also designed Grand Central Terminal. The St. James Theatre's classic design and rich history have made it a cherished landmark in New York City's vibrant theater scene.

The St. James Theatre has a seating capacity of 1,710, offering an intimate yet grand setting for Broadway productions. The theater's interior features elegant decor, including a beautifully adorned proscenium arch and a spacious, comfortable auditorium. The design ensures excellent sightlines and acoustics, providing an optimal experience for theatergoers.

Over the decades, the St. James Theatre has hosted numerous iconic productions and legendary performers. Some of Broadway's most famous shows have graced its stage, including "The King and I," "Hello, Dolly!," "The Producers," and "Oklahoma!." The theater's legacy is deeply intertwined with the history of American musical theater, having been the birthplace of several groundbreaking productions.

One of the St. James Theatre's most notable achievements was hosting the original production of "Oklahoma!" in 1943. This landmark musical by Richard Rodgers and Oscar Hammerstein II revolutionized the genre with its integration of song, dance, and story, setting a new standard for Broadway shows. The success of "Oklahoma!" solidified the St. James Theatre's reputation as a premier venue for musical theater.

In recent years, the St. James Theatre has continued to host acclaimed productions, including the Tony Award-winning musical "The Producers" by Mel Brooks, which set a record for the most Tony Awards ever won by a single show. The theater's commitment to excellence ensures that it remains a vital and dynamic part of Broadway.

The St. James Theatre's historical significance, combined with its ongoing contributions to the theater world, make it a must-visit destination for Broadway enthusiasts. Whether attending a classic musical or a contemporary hit, visitors to the St. James Theatre can expect a memorable and enriching experience in one of New York City's most iconic venues.

Historic Sites

Ellis Island

Ellis Island, located in New York Harbor near the Statue of Liberty, is one of the most significant historic sites in the United States. From 1892 to 1954, Ellis Island served as the primary immigration station for the country, processing over 12 million immigrants seeking a new life in America. Today, the Ellis Island National Museum of Immigration preserves the rich history of this gateway to America and honors the stories of the countless individuals who passed through its halls.

The island's history began long before it became an immigration station. Originally known as Gull Island, it was later called Oyster Island due to the abundant oyster beds in the surrounding waters. In the late 19th century, the federal government took control of immigration from individual states, leading to the establishment of the Ellis Island Immigration Station.

Upon arriving at Ellis Island, immigrants underwent a rigorous inspection process that included medical and legal examinations. The main building, now the museum, was the focal point of this process. Immigrants who passed inspection were free to enter the United States, while those who did not meet the requirements were either treated or sent back to their countries of origin.

The Ellis Island National Museum of Immigration, which opened in 1990, offers a comprehensive and moving exploration of the immigrant experience. The museum's exhibits include photographs, documents, personal belongings, and oral histories that provide a vivid and personal perspective on the journey to America. Interactive displays and multimedia presentations bring to life the challenges and triumphs faced by immigrants.

One of the museum's most poignant features is the American Immigrant Wall of Honor, which lists the names of over 700,000 immigrants and their descendants who passed through Ellis Island. This tribute serves as a powerful reminder of the contributions that immigrants have made to the United States.

Visitors to Ellis Island can also explore the restored Great Hall, where immigrants once waited to be processed. The hall's grandeur and historical significance make it a highlight of any visit.

A visit to Ellis Island is a journey through the history of immigration in America. It offers a profound understanding of the hopes, dreams, and struggles of those who came seeking a better life, making it an essential destination for anyone interested in the nation's diverse heritage.

9/11 Memorial & Museum

The 9/11 Memorial & Museum, located at the World Trade Center site in Lower Manhattan, stands as a poignant tribute to the nearly 3,000 people who lost their lives in the terrorist attacks of September 11, 2001, and the six individuals killed in the 1993 World Trade Center bombing. This sacred site serves as a place of remembrance, reflection, and education, offering a profound and moving experience for visitors from around the world.

The 9/11 Memorial, designed by architect Michael Arad and landscape architect Peter Walker, features two large reflecting pools set within the footprints of the original Twin Towers. Each pool is nearly an acre in size and contains the largest man-made waterfalls in North America. The names of the victims are inscribed on bronze panels surrounding the pools, arranged in a meaningful pattern based on their relationships and locations on the day of the attacks. The serene sound of cascading water and the tranquil atmosphere provide a space for contemplation and mourning.

Adjacent to the memorial, the 9/11 Museum is housed in an architecturally striking building designed by Davis Brody Bond and Snøhetta. The museum's exhibits are located seven stories below ground, within the archaeological remnants of the original World Trade Center. Visitors descend into the museum, passing through the "Survivors' Stairs," which provided a vital escape route for many on 9/11.

The museum's extensive and deeply moving exhibits include artifacts, photographs, and personal stories that document the events of September 11, the aftermath, and the global impact of the attacks. Highlights include the "Last Column," a 36-foot steel beam covered with inscriptions and tributes from first responders and recovery workers, and the "In Memoriam" exhibition, which honors each victim with photographs and biographical information.

The 9/11 Museum also features interactive displays, multimedia presentations, and oral histories that provide a comprehensive understanding of the events and their significance. The "Reflecting on 9/11" exhibition invites visitors to share their own experiences and thoughts, creating a living history of the day.

Visiting the 9/11 Memorial & Museum is a deeply emotional and educational experience that underscores the resilience and strength of the human spirit. It is a place where the memory of those lost is honored, and the lessons of unity, hope, and perseverance are shared with future generations.

St. Patrick's Cathedral

St. Patrick's Cathedral, located on Fifth Avenue between 50th and 51st Streets in Midtown Manhattan, is one of New York City's most iconic and beloved landmarks. As the largest Gothic Revival Catholic cathedral in North America, it serves as the seat of the Archbishop of New York and stands as a symbol of faith, architectural beauty, and historical significance.

The cathedral's construction began in 1858 under the direction of Archbishop John Hughes, who envisioned a grand cathedral to serve the growing Catholic population in New York City. Designed by architect James Renwick Jr., the cathedral's Gothic Revival style is characterized by its pointed arches, intricate stone carvings, and towering spires, which reach a height of 330 feet. The cathedral was officially completed and dedicated in 1879, though additional work, including the addition of the Lady Chapel, continued into the 20th century.

St. Patrick's Cathedral's stunning exterior features a white marble façade, intricate stonework, and an array of statues, including those of saints and biblical figures. The twin spires, added in 1888, are visible from many points in the city and have become a defining feature of the Manhattan skyline.

The interior of the cathedral is equally magnificent, with a grand nave that stretches over 300 feet, soaring vaulted ceilings, and beautiful stained-glass windows that cast colorful light throughout the space. The high altar, designed by architect Charles T. Mathews, is adorned with a bronze baldachin and intricate mosaics, creating a focal point of reverence and beauty.

St. Patrick's Cathedral is not only a place of worship but also a cultural and historical monument. It has hosted numerous significant events, including papal visits, state funerals, and celebrations of major religious and cultural milestones. The cathedral's organ, one of the largest in the country, and its renowned choir contribute to its rich tradition of sacred music.

In recent years, St. Patrick's Cathedral underwent a major restoration project, completed in 2015, to preserve its structural integrity and restore its original splendor. This effort ensured that the cathedral remains a vibrant and welcoming space for worshippers and visitors alike.

St. Patrick's Cathedral's combination of architectural grandeur, historical significance, and spiritual importance make it a must-visit destination in New York City. Whether attending a Mass, exploring its artistic treasures, or simply seeking a moment of quiet reflection, a visit to St. Patrick's Cathedral offers an inspiring and uplifting experience.

Trinity Church

Trinity Church, located at the intersection of Wall Street and Broadway in Lower Manhattan, is one of New York City's oldest and most historically significant landmarks. Established in 1697, the church has been a center of spiritual life and community for over three centuries. Its current Gothic Revival building, designed by architect Richard Upjohn and completed in 1846, stands as a testament to both its historical roots and architectural beauty.

The original Trinity Church was a small parish constructed under the charter granted by King William III of England. It played a crucial role in the early religious and social life of the growing city. The current structure, the third church building on the site, was once the tallest building in the United States until the completion of the New York Tribune Building in 1873. Its 281-foot spire, topped with a gilded cross, remains a striking feature of the Manhattan skyline.

Trinity Church's interior is a serene and ornate space, featuring a grand nave with beautiful stained-glass windows, intricate woodwork, and detailed stone carvings. The reredos, a large altarpiece, and the stunning stained-glass window behind it, depicting scenes from the Bible, add to the church's spiritual and aesthetic allure.

The churchyard at Trinity Church is a historic cemetery where many notable figures from American history are buried. These include

Alexander Hamilton, one of the Founding Fathers and the first Secretary of the Treasury, and Robert Fulton, the inventor of the steamboat. The churchyard offers a quiet, reflective space amidst the bustling financial district and provides a tangible connection to the city's colonial and revolutionary past.

Trinity Church continues to serve as an active parish, offering regular worship services, concerts, and community programs. Its outreach and social justice initiatives address issues such as homelessness, poverty, and education, reflecting its longstanding commitment to service and advocacy.

Visitors to Trinity Church can also explore its rich history through guided tours and educational exhibits. The church's Trinity Museum and Archives house a collection of artifacts and documents that chronicle its significant role in New York City's development.

A visit to Trinity Church offers a blend of historical insight, architectural splendor, and spiritual enrichment, making it a must-see destination for those exploring the rich tapestry of New York City's heritage.

Flatiron Building

The Flatiron Building, an architectural marvel located at 175 Fifth Avenue in the Flatiron District of Manhattan, is one of New York City's most iconic landmarks. Completed in 1902, this triangular, 22-story skyscraper was designed by architect Daniel Burnham and has captivated visitors and residents alike with its unique shape and pioneering design.

The Flatiron Building's distinctive wedge shape, resembling a cast-iron clothes iron, is a result of its location on a triangular parcel of land bounded by Fifth Avenue, Broadway, and East 22nd Street. At its narrowest point, the building is just six feet wide, creating an illusion of even greater height and a striking visual impact. The building's steel-frame construction, a relatively new technique at the time, allowed for its unusual shape and paved the way for future skyscrapers.

The facade of the Flatiron Building is adorned with limestone and terra-cotta detailing, showcasing elements of the Beaux-Arts style. Its elegant design and innovative structure quickly made it a symbol of modernity and architectural progress. The building was originally known as the Fuller Building, named after George A. Fuller, a key figure in the development of skyscraper construction, but it soon became popularly known as the Flatiron Building due to its shape.

The Flatiron Building has been a significant cultural icon since its completion. It has appeared in countless photographs, films, and artworks, contributing to its legendary status. The building's location at the intersection of major thoroughfares also made it a focal point for New York City's early 20th-century urban life. The nearby Flatiron Plaza provides an excellent vantage point for viewing and photographing the building.

Although the Flatiron Building primarily served as office space for much of its history, it has undergone various renovations to preserve its structural integrity and adapt to modern needs. Its lower floors have housed retail spaces and restaurants, adding to the vibrancy of the surrounding neighborhood.

The Flatiron Building's combination of architectural innovation, historical significance, and enduring beauty makes it a must-visit destination in New York City. Whether admired from a distance or explored up close, the Flatiron Building remains a testament to the city's spirit of ingenuity and progress.

New York Public Library (Main Branch)

The New York Public Library's main branch, officially known as the Stephen A. Schwarzman Building, is an iconic cultural and architectural landmark located at Fifth Avenue and 42nd Street in Midtown Manhattan. Opened in 1911, this Beaux-Arts masterpiece serves as a central hub of the New York Public Library system and a treasure trove of knowledge and history.

Designed by architects Carrère and Hastings, the library's exterior is characterized by its grand facade, majestic columns, and ornate sculptures. The building is guarded by two marble lions named Patience and Fortitude, which have become beloved symbols of the institution and the city itself. The library's imposing design and strategic location underscore its importance as a cultural and intellectual epicenter.

Upon entering the library, visitors are greeted by the grand Astor Hall, an expansive marble lobby that sets the tone for the building's opulence and grandeur. The main reading room, the Rose Main Reading Room, is one of the largest of its kind in the world, spanning nearly two city blocks. Its soaring ceilings, magnificent chandeliers, and rows of wooden tables create an inspiring and serene environment for study and reflection.

The library's collections are vast and diverse, encompassing more than 50 million items, including books, manuscripts, maps, photographs, and rare prints. Among its most notable treasures are the Gutenberg Bible, one of the earliest books printed using movable type, and the original manuscript of Charles Dickens' "A Christmas Carol." The library also houses extensive archives related to American history, literature, and culture.

In addition to its rich collections, the New York Public Library offers a wide range of public programs, exhibitions, and educational initiatives. These include author talks, literary events, and special exhibitions that highlight the library's holdings and explore various themes and historical periods. The library's digital collections and online resources extend its reach to a global audience, making its vast resources accessible to researchers and readers around the world.

The New York Public Library's main branch is not only a repository of knowledge but also a vibrant community space that fosters learning, creativity, and intellectual exploration. Whether you are delving into research, attending a cultural event, or simply admiring the architectural splendor, a visit to the New York Public Library offers a deeply enriching and unforgettable experience.

United Nations Headquarters

The United Nations Headquarters, located along the East River in the Turtle Bay neighborhood of Manhattan, is an iconic symbol of international diplomacy and global cooperation. Officially opened in 1952, the complex serves as the central meeting place for the 193 member states of the United Nations (UN). Designed by an international team of architects led by Wallace Harrison, the complex embodies the spirit of unity and peace that the UN represents.

The UN Headquarters comprises several notable buildings, including the General Assembly Hall, the Secretariat Building, and the Security Council Chamber. The General Assembly Hall is the largest and most significant space, where representatives from all member states convene to discuss and address global issues. The Secretariat Building, a sleek, 39-story glass structure, houses the offices of the Secretary-General and other key UN officials. The Security Council Chamber, designed by Norwegian architect

Arnstein Arneberg, features distinctive murals symbolizing the struggle for peace and justice.

Visitors to the United Nations Headquarters can participate in guided tours that offer a behind-the-scenes look at the organization's work and history. These tours provide access to key areas such as the General Assembly Hall, the Security Council Chamber, and the Trusteeship Council Chamber. The tours also include exhibits on various global issues, such as human rights, disarmament, and sustainable development, highlighting the UN's efforts to address these challenges.

The complex is also home to several works of art donated by member states, reflecting the diverse cultures and traditions of the UN's global constituency. Notable pieces include the "Knotted Gun" sculpture, a symbol of non-violence, and Marc Chagall's "Peace Window," a stunning stained-glass work commemorating the ideals of the UN.

The United Nations Headquarters is not just a center for diplomacy but also a cultural and educational destination that promotes understanding and cooperation among nations. Its role in facilitating dialogue and addressing global challenges makes it a vital institution in the quest for peace and development. A visit to the UN Headquarters offers a unique opportunity to witness the workings of international diplomacy and to appreciate the diverse efforts to create a better world.

Federal Hall

Federal Hall, located at 26 Wall Street in the Financial District of Manhattan, is a site of immense historical significance in the United States. Originally constructed in 1703 as New York's City Hall, the building became the nation's first capitol under the newly ratified Constitution. It was here, in 1789, that George Washington took the oath of office as the first President of the United States, marking the beginning of the country's federal government.

The original structure was demolished in 1812, and the current Greek Revival building, designed by architects John Frazee and Ithiel Town, was completed in 1842. This building initially served as the U.S. Custom House for the Port of New York and later as a part of the U.S. Sub-Treasury system. Its majestic columns and grand steps are reminiscent of ancient Greek temples, symbolizing the ideals of democracy and governance.

Today, Federal Hall operates as a museum and memorial, dedicated to preserving and interpreting the history of early American government. Visitors can explore exhibits that detail the events of Washington's inauguration, the creation of the Bill of Rights, and the building's varied uses over the centuries. The site also features a life-size statue of George Washington, which stands on the steps where he was inaugurated, serving as a powerful reminder of the site's historical significance.

Inside, the museum offers a variety of artifacts and exhibits related to the early republic, including a replica of the Bible used during Washington's inauguration and other period documents. The building's rotunda and grand hall provide a fitting backdrop for these displays, adding to the sense of historical gravity.

Federal Hall also hosts educational programs, lectures, and special events that delve into the nation's founding and the principles of democracy. These programs aim to engage visitors of all ages and backgrounds, fostering a deeper understanding of American history and civic responsibility.

A visit to Federal Hall provides a unique opportunity to stand in the very place where pivotal moments in American history unfolded. Its blend of historical exhibits, architectural grandeur, and educational initiatives makes it an essential destination for anyone interested in the roots of the United States' democratic institutions.

Fraunces Tavern Museum

Fraunces Tavern Museum, located at 54 Pearl Street in the Financial District of Manhattan, is one of New York City's oldest and most historically significant landmarks. Established in 1719, the building originally served as a private residence before being converted into a tavern by Samuel Fraunces in 1762. The tavern quickly became a central gathering place for patriots during the American Revolutionary War and played a pivotal role in the early history of the United States.

Fraunces Tavern is perhaps best known for its association with George Washington. On December 4, 1783, following the British evacuation of New York City, Washington delivered his famous farewell address to his officers in the Long Room of the tavern, marking the end of the Revolutionary War. This emotional event is commemorated within the museum, and visitors can see a replica of the room as it appeared at that historic moment.

The Fraunces Tavern Museum, established in 1907, occupies several floors of the original building and offers a rich array of exhibits related to the American Revolution and early American history. The museum's collection includes artifacts such as period clothing, weapons, documents, and paintings, which provide a vivid picture of life during the Revolutionary era.

One of the highlights of the museum is the Long Room, where Washington's farewell took place. The room has been meticulously restored to its 18th-century appearance, offering visitors a tangible connection to the past. Other notable exhibits include the Clinton Dining Room, named after New York Governor George Clinton, and the Tallmadge Room, which showcases artifacts related to Major Benjamin Tallmadge, Washington's chief intelligence officer.

In addition to its permanent exhibits, Fraunces Tavern Museum hosts temporary exhibitions, lectures, and educational programs that explore various aspects of Revolutionary War history and early American life. These programs are designed to engage visitors of all ages and backgrounds, fostering a deeper understanding of the nation's founding.

The museum is also part of the Fraunces Tavern Historic Block, a group of preserved 18th-century buildings that provide a glimpse into colonial New York. The surrounding area, rich in history and charm, enhances the experience of visiting the museum.

Fraunces Tavern Museum's blend of historical artifacts, immersive exhibits, and educational initiatives make it a must-visit destination for history enthusiasts. It offers a unique and engaging window into the revolutionary spirit and the early days of the United States.

Brooklyn Historical Society

The Brooklyn Historical Society, now part of the Center for Brooklyn History, is a premier institution dedicated to preserving and sharing the rich history of Brooklyn. Located at 128 Pierrepont Street in Brooklyn Heights, the society was founded in 1863 and has since become a vital resource for understanding the borough's diverse past and dynamic present.

The society's home is a magnificent Queen Anne-style building, designed by architect George B. Post and completed in 1881. This landmark building features stunning architectural details, including a grand staircase, intricate woodwork, and stained-glass windows, providing an inviting and historically significant setting for its collections and exhibitions.

The Brooklyn Historical Society's vast archives include an extensive collection of photographs, maps, manuscripts, newspapers, and artifacts that document Brooklyn's history from its earliest days to the present. These materials cover a wide range of topics, including immigration, industry, social movements, and everyday life, offering a comprehensive and nuanced view of the borough's development.

One of the society's key exhibits is "Brooklyn Abolitionists/In Pursuit of Freedom," which explores Brooklyn's important role in the abolitionist movement and the fight against slavery. The exhibit highlights the stories of local activists, both black and white, who worked tirelessly to promote freedom and equality. Through documents, artifacts, and interactive displays, visitors gain insight into this critical chapter of American history.

The Brooklyn Historical Society also offers a variety of public programs, including lectures, panel discussions, walking tours, and workshops. These programs engage the community and provide opportunities for lifelong learning. The society's educational initiatives, such as school programs and teacher resources, aim to inspire a love of history in younger generations and promote critical thinking and civic engagement.

In addition to its permanent location, the Brooklyn Historical Society operates the DUMBO location, which focuses on the history and culture of Brooklyn's waterfront. This site hosts exhibitions and events that explore the borough's maritime heritage and the ongoing transformation of its waterfront areas.

The Brooklyn Historical Society's commitment to preserving and sharing the borough's history makes it an invaluable institution for residents and visitors alike. Its rich collections, engaging exhibits, and diverse programs offer a deep and meaningful connection to Brooklyn's past, while also highlighting its ongoing evolution and cultural vibrancy.

Observation Decks

Top of the Rock Observation Deck

The Top of the Rock Observation Deck, located at Rockefeller Center in Midtown Manhattan, offers one of the most breathtaking panoramic views of New York City. Situated atop the 30 Rockefeller Plaza, this iconic observation deck provides an unparalleled vantage point, giving visitors a unique perspective of the city's stunning skyline.

The journey to the Top of the Rock begins with a visit to the stylishly designed entrance and lobby, where visitors can learn about the history and significance of Rockefeller Center through multimedia exhibits. The high-speed glass elevators whisk guests up to the 67th, 69th, and 70th floors, where the observation decks are located.

Each of the three levels offers different experiences and views. The 67th floor features indoor and outdoor viewing areas, equipped with informative displays that highlight key landmarks and points of interest. The 69th floor provides outdoor terraces with glass safety panels, allowing unobstructed views of the city while maintaining visitor safety. The 70th floor, the highest level, boasts an open-air deck without any barriers, offering a 360-degree view of New York City's skyline.

From the Top of the Rock, visitors can see some of the city's most famous landmarks, including the Empire State Building, Central Park, the Chrysler Building, the Brooklyn Bridge, and the Statue of Liberty. The view of Central Park is particularly impressive, providing a striking contrast between the urban landscape and the expansive green space.

The observation deck is also a popular spot for capturing spectacular sunset views, as the city is bathed in golden light, transitioning into the twinkling lights of the evening skyline. The deck remains open until midnight, offering stunning nighttime views as well.

In addition to its stunning views, the Top of the Rock often hosts special events and activities, such as sunrise yoga sessions and stargazing nights, adding unique experiences for visitors.

A visit to the Top of the Rock Observation Deck is a must for anyone wanting to experience the beauty and grandeur of New York City from above. Its central location, historical significance, and unmatched views make it an essential stop on any trip to the Big Apple.

Empire State Building Observatory

The Empire State Building Observatory, located in the heart of Midtown Manhattan, is one of the most iconic and visited attractions in New York City. This Art Deco masterpiece, completed in 1931, was the tallest building in the world at the time and remains a symbol of American ingenuity and architectural excellence.

Visitors to the Empire State Building can explore two main observation decks: the 86th-floor open-air observatory and the 102nd-floor enclosed observatory. The experience begins with an engaging and informative exhibit on the building's history and construction, including the daring feats of the workers who built it and its role in popular culture. The exhibits also highlight the building's sustainability efforts and its iconic status in the New York City skyline.

The 86th-floor observatory, standing 1,050 feet above the city streets, offers a spacious outdoor deck with 360-degree views of New York City and beyond. From this vantage point, visitors can see Central Park, the Statue of Liberty, Times Square, the Brooklyn Bridge, and the Hudson and East Rivers. The observatory is equipped with high-powered binoculars and informative plaques that help identify key landmarks, enhancing the viewing experience.

For those seeking an even higher perspective, the 102nd-floor observatory, located 1,250 feet above ground, offers an enclosed viewing area with floor-to-ceiling windows. This level provides a more intimate and elevated view of the city, making it a popular choice for visitors looking to capture stunning photographs and enjoy a quieter, more serene atmosphere.

The Empire State Building Observatory is open daily, including holidays, and extends its hours into the late evening, allowing visitors to experience the city both day and night. The nighttime views, with the city's twinkling lights and illuminated landmarks, offer a magical and romantic perspective of New York.

In addition to its observatories, the Empire State Building hosts special events and themed nights, including live music performances and seasonal light displays, adding to its appeal as a dynamic and vibrant destination.

A visit to the Empire State Building Observatory is an unforgettable experience that offers unparalleled views of New York City and a deep appreciation for one of the world's most famous skyscrapers. Its combination of historical significance, architectural beauty, and breathtaking vistas make it a must-see attraction for anyone exploring the city.

One World Observatory

One World Observatory, located at the top of One World Trade Center in Lower Manhattan, offers visitors a profound and awe-inspiring view of New York City from the tallest building in the Western Hemisphere. Standing at 1,776 feet, One World Trade Center is not only a symbol of resilience and renewal but also provides an unparalleled vantage point for experiencing the city's grandeur.

The journey to One World Observatory begins with a high-speed elevator ride known as the Sky Pod, which ascends to the 102nd floor in just 47 seconds. During the ascent, floor-to-ceiling LED screens in the elevators showcase a time-lapse video of New York City's skyline evolving over centuries, providing an engaging prelude to the main event.

Upon reaching the top, visitors are greeted by the See Forever Theater, a brief immersive experience that captures the essence and energy of New York City through stunning visuals and sound. The theater's walls then part, dramatically revealing the main observatory and its breathtaking views.

The observatory spans the 100th, 101st, and 102nd floors, offering different perspectives and experiences. The 100th floor, known as the Discovery Level, features expansive floor-to-ceiling windows that provide 360-degree views of the city, including landmarks such as the Statue of Liberty, the Empire State Building, Central Park, and the Brooklyn Bridge. Interactive displays and guides help visitors identify and learn more about the sights below.

One of the standout features of One World Observatory is the Sky Portal, a 14-foot-wide circular glass floor that provides a unique perspective of the streets below. Visitors can step onto the Sky Portal and experience the sensation of looking directly down from the top of the tallest building in the Western Hemisphere.

The 101st floor houses the observatory's dining options, including a sit-down restaurant, bar, and café, allowing visitors to enjoy a meal or drink while taking in the stunning views. The 102nd floor offers exclusive event space and a more intimate viewing experience.

One World Observatory also hosts special events and experiences, such as sunrise yoga sessions and holiday-themed activities, making it a versatile and dynamic destination.

A visit to One World Observatory is both a visual and emotional experience, offering unparalleled views of New York City and a deep connection to the site's historical significance. It stands as a testament to the city's resilience and spirit, providing an unforgettable experience for all who visit.

Edge at Hudson Yards

Edge at Hudson Yards, located on the 100th floor of 30 Hudson Yards, is the highest outdoor sky deck in the Western Hemisphere. Offering a thrilling and unparalleled vantage point, Edge provides visitors with breathtaking views of New York City from 1,131 feet above the ground. Opened in March 2020, it quickly became one of the city's most popular attractions, combining architectural innovation with stunning vistas.

The journey to Edge begins with a dynamic multimedia experience that introduces visitors to the construction and design of Hudson Yards, a vibrant new neighborhood built over a working rail yard. Upon reaching the sky deck, guests are greeted by a sprawling outdoor platform that extends 80 feet from the building, offering a unique perspective over Manhattan and beyond.

One of the standout features of Edge is its glass floor, which allows visitors to look straight down to the streets below. This thrilling experience is not for the faint-hearted, but it provides an unmatched view of the city from a vertigo-inducing height. The sky deck also features angled glass walls, enabling visitors to lean out and feel as if they are floating above the city.

The panoramic views from Edge encompass the entirety of New York City's skyline, including iconic landmarks such as the Empire State Building, Central Park, the Statue of Liberty, and the Hudson River. On clear days, the visibility extends for miles, offering a stunning perspective of the city's vast expanse.

Edge also boasts a champagne bar where visitors can enjoy a drink while taking in the breathtaking scenery. The bar offers a selection of beverages and light snacks, adding a touch of luxury to the experience. Special events and seasonal activities, such as sunrise yoga and holiday celebrations, further enhance the appeal of Edge.

The design and engineering of Edge reflect Hudson Yards' commitment to innovation and sustainability. The sky deck is constructed with state-of-the-art materials and techniques, ensuring both safety and environmental efficiency.

A visit to Edge at Hudson Yards is a must for anyone seeking an exhilarating and unforgettable experience in New York City. Its combination of architectural brilliance, thrilling perspectives, and stunning views make it a standout destination that captures the essence of modern urban innovation.

The High Line

The High Line is a unique urban park and green space that stretches 1.45 miles along Manhattan's West Side. Built on a historic elevated rail line, the park runs from Gansevoort Street in the Meatpacking District to 34th Street near Hudson Yards, offering a captivating blend of nature, art, and city views. Since its opening in 2009, the High Line has become one of New York City's most beloved public spaces, attracting millions of visitors each year.

The High Line's transformation from an abandoned railway to a vibrant park is a remarkable story of community activism and innovative urban design. In the late 1990s, a group of local residents and advocates, known as Friends of the High Line, campaigned to save the deteriorating structure from demolition and repurpose it as a public park. Their efforts culminated in a collaborative design process led by landscape architecture firm James Corner Field Operations and architecture firm Diller Scofidio + Renfro.

Walking along the High Line, visitors encounter a diverse array of plants, trees, and flowers that change with the seasons, creating a dynamic and ever-evolving landscape. The park's design incorporates elements of the original rail tracks, seamlessly blending the old with the new and preserving a sense of the site's industrial heritage.

In addition to its lush greenery, the High Line features numerous art installations and sculptures that enhance the visitor experience. These rotating exhibits showcase the work of contemporary artists and provide thought-provoking and visually engaging elements throughout the park.

The High Line also offers a variety of public programs and events, including guided tours, horticulture workshops, and cultural performances. These activities encourage community engagement and provide opportunities for learning and enrichment.

Several seating areas and observation points along the High Line offer stunning views of the city and the Hudson River. Notable highlights include the 10th Avenue Square and Overlook, a stepped seating area with a glass wall that provides a unique perspective on the bustling street below, and the Chelsea Market Passage, which features food vendors and art exhibitions.

A visit to the High Line is a delightful escape from the urban hustle, offering a peaceful and scenic walkway elevated above the streets of Manhattan. Its combination of natural beauty, artistic expression, and historical significance makes it a must-visit destination for locals and tourists alike.

Roosevelt Island Tramway

The Roosevelt Island Tramway, an iconic and unique mode of transportation in New York City, offers passengers a breathtaking aerial view of the city as it travels between Manhattan and Roosevelt Island. Since its opening in 1976, the tramway has become a beloved and practical part of the city's transit system, providing a quick and scenic route across the East River.

The tramway operates between the tram stations at 59th Street and Second Avenue in Manhattan and Tramway Plaza on Roosevelt Island. Each tram car can accommodate up to 125 passengers and makes the journey in just three minutes, offering stunning vistas of the East River, the Manhattan skyline, and the iconic Queensboro Bridge.

One of the most appealing aspects of the Roosevelt Island Tramway is the unparalleled view it provides. As the tram ascends above the East River, passengers are treated to a sweeping panorama of New York City, including landmarks such as the Chrysler Building, the Empire State Building, and the United Nations Headquarters. The experience is particularly magical during sunset or at night when the city's lights create a mesmerizing backdrop.

The tramway is a vital link for the residents of Roosevelt Island, providing them with easy access to Manhattan's amenities and services. It operates 365 days a year, running every 7-15 minutes, ensuring a reliable and efficient service for commuters and visitors alike. The fare for the tramway is the same as a subway ride, and passengers can use their MetroCard for payment, making it an accessible and affordable option.

Roosevelt Island itself is a destination worth exploring. The island offers a mix of residential, recreational, and historical attractions. Notable sites include the Franklin D. Roosevelt Four Freedoms Park, a serene and beautifully designed memorial at the island's southern tip, and the historic Blackwell House, one of the oldest structures in New York City.

In addition to its practical benefits, the Roosevelt Island Tramway is a tourist attraction in its own right. It has been featured in numerous films and television shows, further cementing its status as a New York City icon.

A ride on the Roosevelt Island Tramway offers a unique and memorable perspective of the city, blending the convenience of urban transit with the thrill of an aerial adventure. It is an essential experience for anyone looking to see New York City from a different vantage point.

Summit One Vanderbilt

Summit One Vanderbilt, located at 1 Vanderbilt Avenue adjacent to Grand Central Terminal, is one of New York City's newest and most exhilarating observation decks. Opened in October 2021, Summit One Vanderbilt offers a multi-sensory experience that combines breathtaking views with immersive art installations and cutting-edge design, elevating the typical observation deck visit to new heights.

Perched atop the 1,401-foot One Vanderbilt skyscraper, Summit One Vanderbilt spans three levels, starting from the 91st floor and culminating in an open-air terrace on the 93rd floor. The journey to the summit begins with a high-speed elevator ride that transports visitors to the heart of the experience. As the doors open, guests are greeted by "Air," an interactive art installation by Kenzo Digital that features mirrored floors, walls, and ceilings, creating a surreal and infinite landscape that reflects the cityscape in dazzling, kaleidoscopic patterns.

The main observation deck offers panoramic views of New York City, including iconic landmarks such as the Empire State Building, Central Park, the Chrysler Building, and the Hudson River. The floor-to-ceiling windows provide an unobstructed, 360-degree view, allowing visitors to take in the city's beauty from all angles.

One of the standout features of Summit One Vanderbilt is the outdoor terrace on the 93rd floor. This open-air space offers a thrilling perspective, with glass panels allowing visitors to lean out and feel as though they are floating above the city. The terrace also includes a unique glass-floor experience called "Levitation," where guests can step out onto transparent floors that extend beyond the building's edge, offering a vertigo-inducing view of the streets far below.

Summit One Vanderbilt also features "Ascent," a glass-enclosed elevator that travels along the exterior of the building, providing an exhilarating ride to the highest point of the observatory. This experience offers unparalleled views and a sense of adventure, making it a highlight for many visitors.

The combination of cutting-edge design, immersive art, and spectacular views makes Summit One Vanderbilt a must-visit destination in New York City. Whether you're a local or a tourist, the experience offers a unique and unforgettable perspective on the city's skyline.

Brooklyn Heights Promenade

The Brooklyn Heights Promenade, also known simply as the Promenade, is a cherished urban oasis that offers stunning panoramic views of the Manhattan skyline, the East River, and the iconic Brooklyn Bridge. Stretching along the waterfront in the historic Brooklyn Heights neighborhood, this pedestrian walkway provides a serene and picturesque setting for both locals and visitors to enjoy.

The Promenade was conceived in the mid-20th century as part of the construction of the Brooklyn-Queens Expressway (BQE). City planner Robert Moses envisioned a dual-purpose structure: a vital roadway with a scenic pedestrian path above it. The result is a beautifully landscaped esplanade that has become one of Brooklyn's most beloved destinations since its completion in the 1950s.

The Promenade's elevated position offers unobstructed views of Lower Manhattan's skyline, including landmarks such as the Freedom Tower, the

Statue of Liberty, and the Empire State Building in the distance. The sight of the sun setting behind the Manhattan skyline, casting a warm glow over the city, is particularly magical and draws photographers and romantics alike.

The walkway is lined with benches, lush greenery, and seasonal flower beds, creating a peaceful retreat from the bustling city streets. It's a popular spot for leisurely strolls, jogging, and simply sitting to take in the views. Families, couples, and solo visitors all find solace in this urban sanctuary, making it a vibrant yet tranquil space.

The Promenade also offers access to nearby attractions. The adjacent Brooklyn Bridge Park extends along the waterfront, featuring playgrounds, sports facilities, and cultural events. The historic brownstone streets of Brooklyn Heights, with their charming architecture and tree-lined avenues, provide a delightful backdrop and are worth exploring.

Throughout the year, the Promenade hosts various community events and celebrations, adding to its role as a social and cultural hub in Brooklyn. It's a place where the local community and visitors come together to enjoy the beauty of the city and the natural world.

The Brooklyn Heights Promenade's blend of scenic beauty, historical significance, and community spirit makes it a must-visit destination. Whether for a morning jog, a leisurely afternoon walk, or an evening of skyline gazing, the Promenade offers an experience that captures the essence of New York City's charm.

Liberty State Park (views of Manhattan skyline)

Liberty State Park, located in Jersey City, New Jersey, offers some of the most spectacular views of the Manhattan skyline, the Statue of Liberty, and Ellis Island. Spanning over 1,200 acres along the Hudson River waterfront, this expansive park is a favorite destination for locals and tourists seeking a tranquil retreat with unparalleled vistas of New York City.

Opened in 1976 as part of the United States Bicentennial celebrations, Liberty State Park was developed on reclaimed land that had previously been used for rail yards and industrial purposes. Today, it stands as a testament to successful urban renewal and environmental conservation, providing a green oasis amidst the urban landscape.

The park's prime location directly across the river from Lower Manhattan offers visitors breathtaking panoramic views of the city skyline. The Liberty Science Center, located within the park, provides an educational experience with interactive exhibits and an impressive IMAX theater, making it a great stop for families and science enthusiasts.

One of the park's most iconic features is Liberty Walk, a picturesque waterfront promenade that stretches for miles along the Hudson River. The walkway offers unobstructed views of the Statue of Liberty and Ellis Island, as well as the skyscrapers of Lower Manhattan. Benches and viewing areas along Liberty Walk provide perfect spots to sit and admire the scenery, take photographs, or simply relax and enjoy the fresh air.

Liberty State Park is also home to the Liberty Landing Marina, which offers boat rentals, dining options, and a public boat launch. The marina's restaurants, with outdoor seating, provide a delightful dining experience with stunning views of the skyline.

The park's open spaces, picnic areas, and playgrounds make it an ideal destination for family outings, picnics, and recreational activities. The Central Railroad of New Jersey Terminal, a historic transportation hub, adds a touch of history to the park and serves as the departure point for ferries to the Statue of Liberty and Ellis Island.

Throughout the year, Liberty State Park hosts various events, festivals, and concerts that draw visitors from both New Jersey and New York. The Fourth of July fireworks display, set against the backdrop of the Manhattan skyline, is particularly popular.

Liberty State Park's combination of natural beauty, recreational amenities, and stunning views of the Manhattan skyline makes it a must-visit destination for anyone looking to experience the best of both New Jersey and New York City. Whether for a day of exploration or a moment of quiet reflection, the park offers a unique and memorable experience.

Neighborhood Exploration

Greenwich Village

Greenwich Village, often simply referred to as "The Village," is one of New York City's most storied and vibrant neighborhoods. Located in Lower Manhattan, it is bounded by Broadway to the east, the Hudson River to the west, Houston Street to the south, and 14th Street to the north. The Village is renowned for its bohemian culture, historic brownstones, and lively arts scene.

Historically, Greenwich Village has been a haven for artists, writers, and intellectuals. In the early 20th century, it was the epicenter of the Beat Generation and later became a hub for the counterculture movement of the 1960s. This rich cultural heritage is still evident today in the neighborhood's numerous theaters, jazz clubs, and cafes. Venues like the Blue Note and Village Vanguard continue to attract jazz enthusiasts from around the world, while Off-Broadway theaters such as the Cherry Lane Theatre keep the area's avant-garde spirit alive.

Washington Square Park, located in the heart of Greenwich Village, is a central gathering place for locals and visitors alike. Its iconic arch, lively street performers, and vibrant atmosphere make it a quintessential part of the neighborhood's charm. The park is also adjacent to New York University (NYU), adding a youthful energy to the area.

Greenwich Village is also known for its diverse and eclectic dining scene. From cozy cafes and bakeries to upscale restaurants and iconic pizza joints like Joe's Pizza, there is something to satisfy every palate. Bleecker Street, in particular, is lined with unique shops, vintage stores, and specialty food markets.

The Village's historic architecture is another highlight, with tree-lined streets and beautifully preserved townhouses that evoke a sense of old New York. The neighborhood's commitment to preserving its historic character is evident in the numerous landmarked buildings and its inclusion in the Greenwich Village Historic District.

Greenwich Village's combination of cultural richness, historic charm, and vibrant community makes it one of New York City's most beloved neighborhoods. Whether you're exploring its artistic venues, enjoying a leisurely stroll through its picturesque streets, or savoring its diverse culinary offerings, Greenwich Village offers a unique and unforgettable experience.

SoHo

SoHo, short for "South of Houston Street," is a dynamic and fashionable neighborhood in Lower Manhattan known for its trendy boutiques, art galleries, and cast-iron architecture. Bounded by Houston Street to the north, Canal Street to the south, Crosby Street to the east, and West Broadway to the west, SoHo has evolved from an industrial area to one of New York City's most vibrant cultural and commercial hubs.

In the mid-20th century, SoHo was primarily an industrial zone with factories and warehouses. However, by the 1960s and 1970s, the neighborhood began to attract artists who were drawn to the large, open spaces of its lofts. These artists transformed SoHo into a thriving arts district, establishing numerous galleries and studios. The area's unique cast-iron buildings, characterized by their intricate facades and expansive windows, provided ideal spaces for creative work and exhibitions.

Today, SoHo is synonymous with high-end shopping and cutting-edge fashion. The neighborhood boasts an array of designer boutiques, flagship stores, and independent shops. Streets like Prince, Spring, and West Broadway are lined with a mix of luxury brands, trendy retailers, and one-of-a-kind boutiques. This retail renaissance has made SoHo a premier shopping destination for fashion enthusiasts from around the world.

Art remains a central element of SoHo's identity. The neighborhood is home to numerous contemporary art galleries, showcasing works by both established and emerging artists. Notable galleries include the Donald Judd Foundation, which preserves the artist's former residence and studio, and the Drawing Center, dedicated to the exhibition of historical and contemporary drawings.

SoHo's culinary scene is equally impressive, offering a diverse range of dining options. From chic cafes and bistros to upscale restaurants and food markets, the neighborhood caters to a variety of tastes and preferences. Popular spots include Balthazar, a bustling French brasserie, and Dominique Ansel Bakery, famous for its inventive pastries.

The neighborhood's historic charm is preserved through its meticulously restored buildings and cobblestone streets. Walking through SoHo, one can appreciate the blend of old and new, where contemporary culture thrives within a backdrop of architectural history.

SoHo's fusion of art, fashion, and culinary delights, combined with its unique architectural heritage, makes it one of New York City's most captivating neighborhoods. Whether you're exploring its galleries, indulging in retail therapy, or savoring gourmet cuisine, SoHo offers an unparalleled urban experience.

Harlem

Harlem, located in Upper Manhattan, is a neighborhood rich in history, culture, and tradition. Bounded by the Harlem River to the north and east, 155th Street to the south, and Morningside Park and St. Nicholas Avenue to the west, Harlem has long been a significant cultural and political hub for African Americans. Its vibrant arts scene, historic landmarks, and diverse community make it one of New York City's most dynamic neighborhoods.

Harlem is perhaps best known for its pivotal role in the Harlem Renaissance, a cultural and artistic movement that flourished in the 1920s and 1930s. This period saw a remarkable outpouring of creativity from African American artists, writers, musicians, and intellectuals. Icons such as Langston Hughes, Zora Neale Hurston, Duke Ellington, and Louis Armstrong contributed to Harlem's reputation as a center of artistic innovation and cultural expression.

The neighborhood's rich musical heritage continues to thrive today. The Apollo Theater, a historic venue on 125th Street, remains a beacon of African American culture and has hosted legendary performers such as Billie Holiday, James Brown, and Aretha Franklin. The theater's Amateur Night, which launched the careers of many famous artists, is still a popular event.

Harlem is also home to a variety of cultural institutions that celebrate its heritage. The Studio Museum in Harlem showcases contemporary African American art, while the Schomburg Center for Research in Black Culture offers extensive archives and exhibitions related to the African diaspora. These institutions, along with numerous community centers and galleries, ensure that Harlem's cultural legacy is preserved and celebrated.

The neighborhood's dining scene is a reflection of its diverse cultural influences. Harlem is renowned for its soul food restaurants, such as Sylvia's and Red Rooster, which offer traditional Southern cuisine with a contemporary twist. Additionally, the area boasts a range of international eateries, reflecting the multicultural makeup of its residents.

Harlem's historic architecture is another highlight. The neighborhood features beautiful brownstones, pre-war buildings, and historic churches that add to its charm. Landmarks such as the Abyssinian Baptist Church and the Hamilton Grange National Memorial offer glimpses into Harlem's storied past.

Harlem's blend of cultural vibrancy, historical significance, and community spirit make it a unique and compelling neighborhood. Whether exploring its artistic landmarks, enjoying live music, or savoring its culinary offerings, visitors to Harlem are sure to experience the rich tapestry of its heritage and vitality.

Williamsburg

Williamsburg, located in Brooklyn, is one of New York City's trendiest and most eclectic neighborhoods. Bounded by the East River to the west, Bushwick Avenue to the east, Flushing Avenue to the south, and McCarren Park to the north, Williamsburg has transformed from an industrial hub into a vibrant cultural and artistic enclave. Its dynamic blend of old and new, along with its diverse community, makes Williamsburg a unique and exciting destination.

Historically, Williamsburg was an industrial center, with factories and warehouses dominating the landscape. However, in the late 20th century, artists and creatives began to move into the neighborhood, attracted by the affordable loft spaces and gritty charm. This influx of creative energy sparked a wave of gentrification, leading to the development of trendy boutiques, art galleries, and innovative restaurants.

Today, Williamsburg is known for its thriving arts scene. The neighborhood is home to numerous galleries, studios, and performance spaces, showcasing works by both emerging and established artists. Venues like the Brooklyn Art Library and the Wythe Hotel's art gallery offer a glimpse into the local creative community. Additionally, street art and murals adorn many of Williamsburg's buildings, adding to its vibrant, urban aesthetic.

Williamsburg's music scene is equally renowned, with venues such as the Music Hall of Williamsburg, Brooklyn Steel, and Rough Trade NYC hosting live performances by a diverse array of artists. From indie rock and electronic music to hip-hop and jazz, the neighborhood's music offerings cater to a wide range of tastes.

The neighborhood's dining scene is a major draw, featuring an array of innovative and eclectic restaurants, cafes, and bars. From Michelin-starred establishments like Aska to casual eateries and food trucks, Williamsburg offers a culinary adventure for food enthusiasts. The area is also known for its artisanal food markets, such as Smorgasburg, which showcase local vendors and unique culinary creations.

Williamsburg's shopping scene is characterized by its mix of independent boutiques, vintage shops, and high-end retailers. Bedford Avenue, the neighborhood's main thoroughfare, is lined with an array of shops offering everything from designer fashion and handmade jewelry to vinyl records and quirky home decor.

In addition to its cultural and commercial offerings, Williamsburg boasts beautiful waterfront parks and green spaces. Domino Park, located along the East River, features stunning views of the Manhattan skyline, recreational facilities, and public art installations.

Williamsburg's blend of creativity, culture, and community makes it one of New York City's most dynamic neighborhoods. Whether exploring its art galleries, enjoying live music, dining at trendy restaurants, or shopping at unique boutiques, visitors to Williamsburg are sure to be captivated by its energetic and eclectic vibe.

Chinatown

New York City's Chinatown is one of the largest and oldest in the United States, centered around Mott, Canal, and Mulberry Streets. Established in the mid-19th century by Chinese immigrants, Chinatown has grown into a bustling neighborhood that preserves its cultural traditions while embracing the city's dynamic urban landscape.

Chinatown is renowned for its vibrant street markets, where vendors sell fresh produce, seafood, spices, and traditional Chinese goods. The neighborhood's many restaurants offer an array of authentic Chinese cuisines, from dim sum and Peking duck to hand-pulled noodles and regional specialties. Popular dining spots include Jing Fong, Joe's

Shanghai, and Nom Wah Tea Parlor, the latter being the city's oldest dim sum restaurant.

In addition to its culinary offerings, Chinatown boasts numerous cultural landmarks and attractions. The Museum of Chinese in America (MOCA) provides a comprehensive overview of the Chinese American experience, with exhibits on immigration, community life, and cultural contributions. The Mahayana Buddhist Temple, with its impressive golden Buddha statue, offers a serene retreat amidst the neighborhood's bustling streets.

Chinatown's vibrant festivals and events, such as the Lunar New Year Parade and the Autumn Moon Festival, draw large crowds and celebrate the neighborhood's rich cultural heritage. These events feature traditional performances, lion dances, and colorful decorations, creating a lively and festive atmosphere.

Little Italy

Little Italy, located just north of Chinatown, is a historic neighborhood that celebrates the legacy of Italian immigrants who settled in New York City in the late 19th and early 20th centuries. While the area has seen significant changes over the years, it retains its charming, old-world ambiance and remains a popular destination for its culinary and cultural offerings.

Mulberry Street, the heart of Little Italy, is lined with Italian restaurants, cafes, and bakeries that serve classic dishes such as pasta, pizza, cannoli, and espresso. Notable establishments include Lombardi's, America's first pizzeria, and Ferrara Bakery & Cafe, known for its delicious pastries and gelato.

Little Italy is famous for its annual Feast of San Gennaro, a 10-day street festival held in September that celebrates the patron saint of Naples. The festival features parades, live music, food stalls, and religious processions, attracting visitors from around the world.

The neighborhood also offers a glimpse into its history through landmarks such as the Church of the Most Precious Blood and the Italian American Museum, which documents the contributions of Italian immigrants to the city's cultural fabric.

Chinatown and Little Italy's close proximity allows visitors to easily explore both neighborhoods, experiencing the rich cultural traditions, vibrant street life, and delectable cuisines that define these historic communities. Whether savoring dim sum in Chinatown or enjoying a leisurely meal in Little Italy, visitors can immerse themselves in the diverse and dynamic heritage of New York City.

Upper West Side

The Upper West Side, located between Central Park and the Hudson River from 59th Street to 110th Street, is one of Manhattan's most desirable and family-friendly neighborhoods. Known for its leafy streets, historic brownstones, and vibrant cultural scene, the Upper West Side offers a charming and sophisticated atmosphere.

The neighborhood is home to several iconic institutions, including the American Museum of Natural History, which features extensive exhibits on dinosaurs, human evolution, and outer space. The nearby Hayden Planetarium offers immersive astronomical shows that captivate visitors of all ages. Lincoln Center for the Performing Arts, another cultural landmark, hosts world-class performances by the New York Philharmonic, the Metropolitan Opera, and the New York City Ballet.

Central Park, bordering the Upper West Side to the east, provides residents and visitors with abundant recreational opportunities. Popular spots within the park include the Great Lawn, the Shakespeare Garden, and the Jacqueline Kennedy Onassis Reservoir, ideal for jogging and leisurely strolls.

The Upper West Side boasts a diverse dining scene, with numerous cafes, restaurants, and markets. From upscale dining at establishments like Jean-Georges to casual eats at local favorites like Zabar's and Barney Greengrass, the neighborhood caters to a variety of tastes and preferences.

East Village

The East Village, located between the Bowery and the East River from 14th Street to Houston Street, is a vibrant and eclectic neighborhood known for its artistic heritage, diverse culture, and lively nightlife. Historically a hub for counterculture and bohemian lifestyles, the East Village has maintained its creative spirit while evolving into a trendy and dynamic area.

The neighborhood is famous for its music scene, with legendary venues like Webster Hall and the Bowery Ballroom hosting performances by renowned and emerging artists. The East Village also boasts numerous theaters and performance spaces, such as the La MaMa Experimental Theatre Club, which continues to support innovative and avant-garde productions.

St. Mark's Place, a bustling street lined with shops, cafes, and bars, epitomizes the East Village's eclectic and energetic vibe. The neighborhood's dining scene is equally diverse, offering everything from gourmet cuisine to ethnic eats and late-night snacks. Popular spots include Veselka, a beloved Ukrainian diner, and Momofuku Noodle Bar, known for its inventive takes on ramen.

DUMBO

DUMBO, short for "Down Under the Manhattan Bridge Overpass," is a trendy and picturesque neighborhood in Brooklyn. Bordered by the Brooklyn Bridge, the Manhattan Bridge, and the East River, DUMBO offers stunning waterfront views and a mix of historic and contemporary architecture.

Once an industrial area with factories and warehouses, DUMBO has transformed into a vibrant cultural and creative hub. The neighborhood is home to numerous art galleries, design studios, and tech companies, contributing to its innovative and dynamic atmosphere. The DUMBO Arts Festival, held annually, showcases the work of local artists and attracts visitors from all over the city.

Brooklyn Bridge Park, a waterfront green space with lush lawns, playgrounds, and sports facilities, is a highlight of the neighborhood. The park's various piers offer breathtaking views of the Manhattan skyline and the Brooklyn Bridge, making it a popular spot for photography and leisure.

DUMBO's dining scene is diverse and trendy, with a range of restaurants, cafes, and food markets. Popular establishments include Grimaldi's Pizzeria, known for its coal-fired pizza, and the Time Out Market, which features a curated selection of local food vendors.

Astoria

Astoria, located in the northwestern part of Queens, is a vibrant and diverse neighborhood known for its rich cultural heritage, bustling food scene, and strong sense of community. Bounded by the East River to the west and Steinway Street to the east, Astoria offers a mix of residential streets, commercial avenues, and waterfront parks.

The neighborhood's cultural diversity is reflected in its culinary offerings, with a wide array of restaurants serving Greek, Italian, Middle Eastern, and Latin American cuisines. Astoria's Greek community, in particular, has a strong presence, with numerous Greek tavernas and bakeries dotting the area. Popular spots include Taverna Kyclades for seafood and Titan Foods for traditional Greek products.

Astoria Park, located along the East River, is one of the neighborhood's main attractions. The park features expansive lawns, walking trails, and sports facilities, including the oldest and largest swimming pool in New York City. The park's waterfront promenade offers stunning views of the Manhattan skyline and the Hell Gate Bridge.

Astoria's cultural scene includes the Museum of the Moving Image, dedicated to the history and art of film, television, and digital media. The neighborhood is also home to Kaufman Astoria Studios, one of the city's oldest and most active film and television production facilities.

Food and Dining

Iconic NYC Foods

New York City is famous for its iconic foods, each deeply embedded in the city's culinary fabric and cultural identity. Bagels, pizza, and hot dogs are not just foods in New York—they are institutions, beloved by locals and tourists alike. Each of these quintessential NYC eats has its own unique history and places to find the best versions in the city.

Bagels

New York City's bagels are world-renowned, known for their unique texture—a perfect balance of a chewy interior and a slightly crisp exterior. This distinct texture is credited to the city's water, which is said to have a unique mineral composition that contributes to the bagels' excellence.

Bagels were brought to New York by Eastern European Jewish immigrants in the late 19th and early 20th centuries. Over the years, they have become a staple of the city's breakfast and brunch culture. Traditional New York bagels come in a variety of flavors, such as plain, sesame, poppy seed, and everything, and are typically enjoyed with a schmear of cream cheese, lox (smoked salmon), or other toppings.

Some of the most famous bagel shops in New York include:

- **Ess-a-Bagel:** Known for its large, fluffy bagels and extensive selection of spreads and toppings.
- **Russ & Daughters:** A Lower East Side institution famous for its bagels with lox and other traditional Jewish delicacies.
- **H&H Bagels:** A longstanding favorite offering a classic New York bagel experience.

Pizza

New York-style pizza is another culinary icon, characterized by its thin, foldable crust and generous slices. Originating from the Italian immigrant communities in the early 20th century, New York pizza has become a symbol of the city itself.

The quintessential New York pizza slice is topped with a simple tomato sauce and mozzarella cheese, though toppings vary widely. The key to its distinct flavor lies in the high-gluten flour used for the dough and the traditional coal-fired or gas ovens that cook the pies to perfection.

Some of the most celebrated pizzerias in New York City include:

- **Di Fara Pizza:** Located in Brooklyn, this legendary spot is known for its handcrafted pies made by the owner, Dom DeMarco.
- **Lombardi's:** Recognized as America's first pizzeria, established in 1905, Lombardi's offers a historic and delicious pizza experience.
- **Joe's Pizza:** A Greenwich Village institution famous for its classic New York slices, popular with both locals and celebrities.

Hot Dogs

The New York City hot dog is a street food staple, known for its simplicity and deliciousness. Hot dogs were popularized in the United States by German immigrants in the late 19th century and quickly became a beloved snack in New York.

A classic New York hot dog is typically served with mustard and sauerkraut, though onions and relish are also common toppings. The hot dogs are often sold from street carts, affectionately known as "dirty water dogs" due to the method of boiling the sausages in hot water.

Some iconic spots to grab a hot dog in New York City include:

- **Nathan's Famous:** Founded in Coney Island in 1916, Nathan's is synonymous with the New York hot dog experience. The annual hot dog eating contest held on July 4th is a major event.
- **Gray's Papaya:** Known for its "Recession Special" (two hot dogs and a drink), this iconic stand offers a delicious and affordable New York hot dog experience.

- **Papaya King:** Another legendary hot dog stand, Papaya King is famous for its hot dogs paired with tropical fruit drinks.

Each of these iconic foods—bagels, pizza, and hot dogs—represents a slice of New York City's rich culinary history. Sampling these treats is not just about enjoying great food; it's about experiencing a piece of the city's vibrant culture and traditions.

Fine Dining

New York City is home to some of the world's most renowned fine dining establishments, offering exquisite culinary experiences that attract food enthusiasts from around the globe. The city's fine dining scene is characterized by its diversity, innovation, and the sheer number of Michelin-starred restaurants.

Michelin-Starred Restaurants

New York City boasts an impressive number of Michelin-starred restaurants, representing a wide array of cuisines and styles. These establishments are known for their meticulous attention to detail, exceptional service, and the use of the finest ingredients.

- **Le Bernardin:** A celebrated seafood restaurant by Chef Eric Ripert, Le Bernardin has maintained its three Michelin stars for many years. Known for its elegant, understated ambiance and perfectly executed dishes, it's a must-visit for seafood lovers.
- **Eleven Madison Park:** This three Michelin-starred restaurant offers a seasonal tasting menu that showcases the best local ingredients. Chef Daniel Humm's creative approach to fine dining has earned Eleven Madison Park numerous accolades.
- **Per Se:** Located in the Time Warner Center, Chef Thomas Keller's Per Se features a nine-course tasting menu that reflects his commitment to culinary excellence. The restaurant's stunning views of Central Park add to the exceptional dining experience.

Internationally Inspired Fine Dining

New York's fine dining scene also includes a variety of internationally inspired restaurants that bring global flavors to the city.

- **Masa:** This three Michelin-starred sushi restaurant by Chef Masa Takayama offers an omakase experience that is both intimate and luxurious. With fish flown in daily from Japan, Masa is considered one of the best sushi restaurants in the world.
- **Daniel:** Chef Daniel Boulud's flagship restaurant, Daniel, offers French cuisine with a modern twist. The elegant setting and impeccable service make it a favorite among fine dining aficionados.
- **Jean-Georges:** Situated at the Trump International Hotel, Jean-Georges Vongerichten's eponymous restaurant features a menu that blends French, American, and Asian influences. The restaurant's innovative dishes and sophisticated atmosphere have earned it three Michelin stars.

Casual Eateries

New York City's casual eateries offer a more relaxed dining experience without compromising on quality. From neighborhood bistros to trendy cafes, these establishments provide a diverse range of delicious and affordable options.

Neighborhood Favorites

Casual eateries are often neighborhood institutions, beloved by locals for their cozy ambiance and consistently good food.

- **Jack's Wife Freda:** With locations in SoHo and the West Village, Jack's Wife Freda is known for its inviting atmosphere and Mediterranean-inspired menu. Popular dishes include the green shakshuka and the rosewater waffle.

- **Roberta's:** This Bushwick hotspot is famous for its wood-fired pizzas and laid-back vibe. The menu also features a variety of creative small plates and seasonal dishes.
- **Buvette:** A charming French bistro in the West Village, Buvette offers a menu of simple yet delicious dishes like croque monsieur, ratatouille, and coq au vin. Its intimate setting makes it perfect for brunch or a casual dinner.

Trendy Cafes and Diners

New York is also home to a plethora of trendy cafes and diners that serve up everything from classic American fare to innovative brunch dishes.

- **Russ & Daughters Cafe:** Located on the Lower East Side, this offshoot of the legendary appetizing store offers a menu of Jewish-American classics, including bagels with lox, matzo ball soup, and pastrami sandwiches.
- **The Grey Dog:** A popular cafe with several locations, The Grey Dog is known for its hearty breakfast and lunch options, including avocado toast, burgers, and salads. Its cozy, rustic decor adds to its charm.
- **Clinton Street Baking Company:** Famous for its blueberry pancakes, this Lower East Side diner draws crowds for its all-day breakfast and comfort food offerings. The biscuits and fried chicken are also standout dishes.

Street Food and Food Trucks

New York City's street food and food truck scene is vibrant and diverse, offering a quick and delicious way to sample a wide range of cuisines. From hot dog stands to gourmet food trucks, these mobile eateries are an integral part of the city's culinary landscape.

Classic Street Food

The city's classic street food vendors have become iconic symbols of New York's fast-paced lifestyle. In addition to the already mentioned hot dogs, street carts in the city will offer:

- **Pretzels:** Soft pretzels, often sold from carts on busy street corners, are a popular snack. These warm, salty treats are perfect for a quick bite on the go.
- **Halal Carts:** Halal food carts, such as the famous Halal Guys, offer tasty and affordable Middle Eastern fare. Dishes like chicken or lamb over rice with white sauce and pita bread are favorites among locals and tourists alike.

Gourmet Food Trucks

The city's food truck scene has exploded in recent years, with gourmet trucks offering inventive and high-quality dishes from around the world.

- **Korilla BBQ:** This food truck fuses Korean flavors with Mexican street food, serving up delicious dishes like bulgogi burritos and kimchi quesadillas.
- **The Cinnamon Snail:** A popular vegan food truck, The Cinnamon Snail offers a creative menu that includes items like Korean BBQ seitan sandwiches, maple mustard tempeh sandwiches, and indulgent vegan donuts.
- **Big Gay Ice Cream:** Originally a food truck and now a beloved ice cream shop, Big Gay Ice Cream is known for its playful and decadent soft-serve creations. Favorites include the Salty Pimp (vanilla ice cream with dulce de leche, sea salt, and chocolate dip) and the Bea Arthur (vanilla ice cream with dulce de leche and crushed Nilla wafers).

Pop-Up Markets

In addition to individual food trucks, New York hosts several pop-up markets where multiple vendors gather to offer a variety of street food options.

- **Smorgasburg:** As mentioned earlier, Smorgasburg is a weekend food market that features over 100 vendors offering an incredible array of dishes. From ramen burgers to artisanal ice cream, there's something for everyone.
- **Urbanspace Vanderbilt:** This food hall near Grand Central Terminal features a rotating selection of food vendors, offering everything from lobster rolls to sushi burritos.

Whether you're craving a quick snack or a gourmet meal on the go, New York City's street food and food truck scene has something to satisfy every palate. These mobile eateries offer a convenient and delicious way to experience the city's diverse culinary offerings.

Ethnic Cuisine

New York City is a global melting pot, and nowhere is this more evident than in its diverse neighborhoods, each offering a rich tapestry of ethnic cuisines. Little Italy, Chinatown, and Koreatown are three of the most vibrant areas, where visitors can indulge in authentic and delicious foods from around the world.

Little Italy

Little Italy, located in Lower Manhattan, is a historic neighborhood that celebrates the legacy of Italian immigrants who settled in New York City in the late 19th and early 20th centuries. Though the area has evolved over the years, it retains its charming, old-world ambiance and remains a culinary haven for lovers of Italian cuisine.

Mulberry Street, the heart of Little Italy, is lined with Italian restaurants, cafes, and bakeries that serve classic dishes such as pasta, pizza, and cannoli. Notable establishments include Lombardi's, recognized as America's first pizzeria, where visitors can savor a slice of history along with their pie. For a sweet treat, Ferrara Bakery & Cafe, founded in 1892, offers a delightful selection of Italian pastries, gelato, and espresso.

The neighborhood is also famous for its annual Feast of San Gennaro, a 10-day street festival held in September that celebrates the patron saint of

Naples. The festival features parades, live music, food stalls, and religious processions, attracting visitors from around the world. During the feast, Mulberry Street transforms into a lively celebration of Italian culture and cuisine, with vendors selling sausage and peppers, zeppole, and other Italian street foods.

Chinatown

Chinatown, also in Lower Manhattan, is one of the largest and oldest Chinatowns in the United States. Established by Chinese immigrants in the mid-19th century, the neighborhood is a bustling enclave that offers a wide array of authentic Chinese cuisine.

Chinatown's streets are filled with markets, bakeries, and restaurants that showcase the diverse flavors of China. Dim sum, a traditional Cantonese meal of small plates, is a popular choice, with restaurants like Jing Fong and Golden Unicorn offering a variety of dumplings, buns, and other delicacies served from rolling carts. For a more casual bite, Joe's Shanghai is famous for its soup dumplings, a must-try for any visitor.

In addition to Cantonese cuisine, Chinatown also offers dishes from other regions of China. Spicy Sichuan cuisine can be found at restaurants like Han Dynasty, while Xi'an Famous Foods serves dishes inspired by the flavors of China's Shaanxi province, including hand-pulled noodles and spicy lamb burgers.

Chinatown's vibrant food scene is complemented by its lively street markets, where vendors sell fresh produce, seafood, and exotic ingredients. These markets provide a glimpse into the neighborhood's rich culinary traditions and are a must-visit for any food enthusiast.

Koreatown

Koreatown, located around West 32nd Street between Fifth Avenue and Broadway in Midtown Manhattan, is a bustling neighborhood known for its Korean restaurants, bakeries, and karaoke bars. Often referred to as "K-town," this area offers an immersive experience of Korean culture and cuisine.

Koreatown is renowned for its Korean BBQ restaurants, where diners can grill their own meat at the table. Popular spots include Kang Ho Dong Baekjeong and Jongro BBQ, where guests can enjoy a variety of marinated meats, seafood, and vegetables cooked over a charcoal grill. The experience is often complemented by an array of banchan (small side dishes) such as kimchi, pickled radishes, and seasoned spinach.

For those seeking comfort food, Koreatown offers a variety of traditional Korean dishes. BCD Tofu House is famous for its bubbling hot pots of soondubu jjigae (soft tofu stew), while Her Name is Han serves homestyle Korean dishes like bibimbap (mixed rice) and bulgogi (marinated beef). Kimbap, a Korean version of sushi rolls, can be found at Woorijip, a popular spot for quick and tasty Korean snacks.

Koreatown's food scene extends beyond savory dishes to include an array of sweet treats and beverages. Paris Baguette and Tous Les Jours are popular Korean bakeries that offer a delightful selection of pastries, cakes, and bread. For a refreshing dessert, visitors can try bingsu, a Korean shaved ice dessert topped with fruits, condensed milk, and sweet red beans, at places like Grace Street.

In addition to its culinary delights, Koreatown is known for its vibrant nightlife. Karaoke bars, or noraebang, such as Gagopa Karaoke, offer a fun and lively atmosphere where groups can sing their favorite songs in private rooms.

Little Italy, Chinatown, and Koreatown each provide a unique culinary journey, showcasing the rich traditions and flavors of their respective cultures. Exploring these neighborhoods offers a delicious and immersive experience of New York City's diverse food scene.

Food Markets

New York City is renowned for its diverse culinary landscape, and its food markets are some of the best places to experience this gastronomic variety. Among these, Chelsea Market and Smorgasburg stand out as must-visit destinations for food lovers seeking a wide array of flavors and culinary delights.

Chelsea Market

Located in the Meatpacking District at 75 Ninth Avenue, Chelsea Market is one of New York City's most iconic indoor food markets. Housed in a historic building that once served as the National Biscuit Company's factory, the market retains much of its industrial charm with exposed brick walls, iron fixtures, and a lively, bustling atmosphere.

Chelsea Market is a food lover's paradise, offering an eclectic mix of vendors that cater to a wide range of tastes and preferences. Visitors can find everything from artisanal bread and fresh seafood to gourmet chocolates and exotic spices. Popular vendors include The Lobster Place, known for its fresh lobster rolls and seafood offerings, and Sarabeth's Bakery, famous for its pastries and jams.

In addition to its food stalls, Chelsea Market features several sit-down restaurants where visitors can enjoy a full meal. Cull & Pistol Oyster Bar offers a menu focused on fresh seafood, while Los Tacos No. 1 serves some of the best tacos in the city. The market also houses retail shops selling kitchenware, specialty foods, and unique gifts, making it a one-stop destination for both culinary delights and shopping.

Smorgasburg

Smorgasburg, often referred to as "the Woodstock of eating," is an open-air food market that showcases some of the best street food vendors in New York City. Founded in 2011, Smorgasburg has become a beloved weekend tradition, drawing thousands of visitors to its various locations in Brooklyn and Manhattan.

The market operates seasonally, typically from April to October, with its flagship locations at Williamsburg's East River State Park and Prospect Park in Brooklyn. Smorgasburg features over 100 local vendors offering an incredible variety of dishes, from classic comfort foods to innovative culinary creations. Notable vendors include Ramen Burger, known for its unique burger with ramen noodle buns, and Big Mozz, famous for its mozzarella sticks.

One of the highlights of Smorgasburg is the opportunity to sample a diverse array of international cuisines all in one place. Visitors can enjoy everything from Japanese-inspired tacos and Venezuelan arepas to Filipino halo-halo and Italian gelato. The market's lively atmosphere, combined with its scenic waterfront locations, makes it a perfect spot for a leisurely weekend outing.

Both Chelsea Market and Smorgasburg offer unique and memorable culinary experiences, showcasing the best of New York City's vibrant food scene. Whether you're exploring the historic indoor market of Chelsea or indulging in the diverse street food offerings at Smorgasburg, these food markets are essential destinations for any food enthusiast visiting the city.

Made in United States
Troutdale, OR
03/30/2025